December 25, 1975

To Christel –

With our love and best
wishes for a merry Christmas – and many
more in the future.

Happy reading – and riding!

Linda & Pierre

Meet the Horse

Meet

the Horse

by Patricia H. Johnson

illustrated by Walter D. Osborne

Grosset & Dunlap   *Publishers*   New York

*Hackney Horse team, proud possession of the Busch estate in St. Louis. August
Busch, Jr., is the driver and his family are the lucky passengers.*

Copyright © 1967 by Patricia H. Johnson
All rights reserved
Published simultaneously in Canada
Library of Congress Catalog Card Number: 67–24239
Printed in the United States of America
ISBN: 0-448-01148-4 (TRADE EDITION)
ISBN: 0-448-06526-6 (LIBRARY EDITION)
1972 Printing

Contents

His horse is often the only companion of this Park Service ranger as he patrols the remote reaches of Yellowstone Park.

The Horse in History

The horse, above all other creatures put to use by man, has had the greatest effect upon the course of civilization. His association with his human masters has been one of dedicated service in the most important areas of man's life and progress. Yet, despite a history of enduring service, he has never assumed a role of servitude.

The very earliest ancestors of the horse may be traced back to the Jurassic period 160,000,000 years ago when the first warm-blooded fur-bearing creatures dared to brave a world ruled by dinosaurs and the fierce Tyrannosaurus rex.

A descendant of these primitive adventurers was a five-toed mammal called Condylartha which inhabited every continent except Australia. Several offshoots of the Condylartha proved, according to the evidence of fossils, to be rather monstrous creatures in their own right. While these fell into extinction, a rather gentle-natured family of leaf-eating animals, called Hyracotherium, survived into the Paleocene period which ended 60,000,000 years ago. The greater number of Hyracotherium measured from about 10 to 20 inches tall and had four toes, as opposed to the original five of their Condylarth forefathers. One type, however, showed even clearer evidence of the eventual hoof development of the modern horse. This was Eohippus—the "dawn Horse"—a reputedly dull-witted, fox-terrier-sized little beast who laid claim to distinction by possessing hind feet that were equipped with but three toes. This, of course, portends of things to come, for it represents the initial stage of what will emerge as a pattern—namely, a tendency for the middle digit to enlarge while the side toes dwindle and disappear. This, it is thought, resulted from the fact that Eohippus literally had to keep on his toes in order to survive, maintaining a constant vigil against danger since his only defense was swift retreat.

The Eocene era, in which Eohippus developed, endured some 20 million years, and at the next major stage of the horse's evolution he appears in the Oligocene epoch, about 40 million years ago, in the form of Mesohippus. In structure, Mesohippus rather resembles a deer and in size he approaches the proportions of sheep. Of his original five Condylarthal toes, the first has gone altogether and the fifth has shrunk to a vestigial "splint." Of the three remaining digits, the central one is now enlarged, and while each side toe still touches the ground, none but the middle performs any real function. Mesohippus still feeds upon low-hanging leafy trees, but his teeth nevertheless show signs of becoming longer and hardier and his jaws are more obvious.

It is in the Miocene period, which ended some 10 million years ago, that the horse is confronted with a new change in the natural world around him—and here he becomes known as Merychippus. Though perhaps as early as 50 million years ago numerous equine ancestors began migrating to other continents, via land bridges linking Asia to Alaska where the Bering Strait is now, it is known that these creatures were originally native to North America. Similarly to man, the forebears of the horse underwent certain waves of migration which account for fossil findings in other parts of the globe. But all scientific research indicates that he was initially a native of North America and continued to exist here until less than 10,000 years ago. It remains a mystery why this continent was totally devoid of any horse-life whatsoever at the arrival of Spanish conquistadors, who brought horses with them which began to repopulate the country. Depletion of food, glacial avalanches from the ice age, pestilence, the menace of the human hunter—any or all might have extinguished the horse from his primitive habitat. All that is known is that when the Spanish adventurers landed, no horses were here and the Indians, who quickly learned to become accomplished horsemen themselves, were at first overcome with awe and terror at the completely unfamiliar sight of men on horseback.

But to return to the Miocene era, there was Merychippus calmly nibbling on tender leaves in the relative safety of forests that covered the American West when his kind evolved. Then, in the course of thousands of years, cool, dry winds began sifting down from the north, gradually withering the forests to stark, open plains that offered defenseless animals no refuge whatever from attackers. Moreover, tender tidbits of the forest diet were gone forever, and instead there was only what grew along the ground—rough plains grasses. Thus Merychippus was faced with extinc-ton by way of starvation or by becoming meals for meat-eating animals, or survival by way of change. The second alternative prevailed, and indications of his adaptation are unmistakable.

First, there is growth in his over-all size, making him now about as large as a small pony. His neck extends to greater length, permitting him to reach down and crop grass. His teeth are nearly as strong and well developed as those of today's horse, enabling him to chew the tough grasses, and although his two extra toes still appear beside the large central digit, they no longer touch the ground and will soon recede altogether. He is now a good deal swifter, too, for since speed is still his only escape from danger, he is learning to use it well.

It was a fairly easy step from the Miocene era to the Pliocene era,

The horse can be as mannerly as a Lipizzaner (below) from the famous Spanish Academy of Vienna, or as rank as this fighting bucking horse.

in which the horse appears as Pliohippus, for the harshest changes had been accomplished in the earlier period. Pliohippus, who existed until as recently as a million years ago, is very nearly a true and fully developed horse, although small in size. His stature is now equal to that of a large donkey's and each foot is now an actual hoof, without any unnecessary toes.

Now we are ready for Equus—the true wild horse who arrived in the Pleistocene period (the era in which we now live) and resembled the modern horse in almost every way. The few alterations on the form of Equus are the result of man's influence on breeding. Man's interest in improving the species, however, was scarcely evident in the initial meeting between them. There was Equus, too big to hide, indeed too defenseless to do anything at all but run. And there was Man, already toying with such ideas as the wheel, fire and weapons—and possessed of a tremendous appetite that would not be satisfied by a wholly vegetable diet. As the skeletal remains of approximately 100,000 horses discovered at a Cro-Magnon cave in France indicate, primitive man feasted freely on horseflesh.

Fortunately for the survival of Equus, the hungry Homo sapiens progressed from pre-historic tribal ways to the more advanced cultures of early history—and acquired a taste for more advanced interests. There was still hunting, of course, and a kind of fledgling commerce, but most of all there was war. In all of these pursuits, and especially the last, the horse was so valuable that eating him was considered to be ridiculous. Instead, he was trained to carry the mounted warrior and charge to the fore with the battle chariot.

The Hittites, an aggressive people whose origins were in Asia Minor, were a civilization of masterful horsemen who gained much of their knowledge from Aryan neighbors to the southeast. This neighboring tribe was called the Mitanni and apparently had cultural exchanges with India. Translations of Hittite tablets disclose that the Mitanni prescribed excellent methods for the training and conditioning of horses—methods as valid today as they were thousands of years past. Owing to this borrowed knowledge, and the superb use of it by their troops, the Hittites were able to sweep through the Near East, claiming victories over the Assyrians and Babylonians, and finally invade bordering regions of Egypt and Arabia. This was the first use of cavalry and speed by a conquering empire, and its success afforded a lesson soon to be learned by the rest of the world.

Persian horse troops of very high quality were used in the invasion of Greece in 490 B.C. The Persians expected that on the open plain of Marathon the maneuverability of the cavalry would spell disaster for the Greek infantry, and it is likely the Persians would have achieved their aim had not the Greek commander Miltiades outwitted them by trickery and crafty tactics.

The Greeks, however, learned their lesson from this close call and needed no further demonstration of the importance of cavalry, even though the mountainous terrain of their land did not lend itself as well to mounted armies as did the flat, desert countries. Nevertheless, by 336 B.C., when Alexander the Great commanded the Hellenic forces, a superb Greek cavalry had been developed to accompany its battalions of foot soldiers. Alexander, himself a brilliant equestrian and lover of horses, deployed his ranks with pure genius and in his noted battle against Porus (in what is now Kashmir) demonstrated strategy so clever and effective that his methods are still praised by military historians.

The Romans, after having their infantry mauled by Hannibal's mounted soldiers, tried hard to develop an impressive cavalry and succeeded in doing so enough to return the blow. Scipio Africanus, in a second engagement with the Carthaginians, had an army which included horsemen, and these brought Hannibal to defeat. Essentially, however, the Roman legions consisted chiefly of foot soldiers and their generals in command never really acquired the appreciation for horse troops that the Greeks had had. When the Roman infantry fell for good and all, in 378 A.D., it was at the hands of the Goths superbly mounted on heavy northern horses. And this event was to spell the future of military action for the next thousand years and more, for commencing with the fall of Rome, history would be forged almost entirely by the warrior on horseback.

The flower of mounted armies bloomed at its most glorious in the time of the Middle Ages when gleaming knights and cavaliers rode forth on massive charges in armor and blazing heraldry to defend their nations— and, more, their honor. The very word chivalry originates from the French word for horse, *cheval*, and describes all that is most gallant and noble in man on horseback. It was several long centuries before gunpowder and firearms began to make armor useless and brought about a gradual return to lighter type horses, but cavalry tactics remained important. The map of Europe was shaped and reshaped by, for example, Marlborough's success at Blenheim and Frederick the Great's at Rossbach and Zorndorf, and in the American Civil War crucial battles were won by both sides through skillful use of cavalry.

Advances in artillery were destined to come, however, and with the improvement of war machines the horse was made obsolete. Perhaps the first inkling of his decline was at Balaklava when the Charge of the Light Brigade fell to its famous and tragic fate. The final blow occurred in World War II, when history's last mounted troops were massacred by the Germans. Nazi tanks roared into Poland, and the Poles, with virtually no modern defenses at all, mounted their cavalry, mustered their pitiful arms, including antique lances that ornamented the halls of nineteenth-century buildings, and rode out to engage the invaders. They knew, of course, that there wasn't a chance for survival of the onslaught, and even the Nazis were moved by the hopelessness of the attempt. One German soldier noted in his diary that his men began to weep when, amid a blinding snow and bitter, freezing cold, they encountered a Polish trooper on his mount, fixed and motionless in front of them. Man and horse were still upright, frozen to death in the snow.

After nearly 4,000 years of soldiering, the horse had come to the end of his military career. He now is used full-time in what were once only minor duties—giving and sharing pleasure, providing excitement and admiration as a star of the sporting arena, and performing peaceful tasks where his steadfast service is still irreplaceable. To delight our sporting instincts, to fulfill our need for both relaxation and adventure, and to handle the jobs where he's still required as a working tool, a wide variety of horse breeds exists. Most of them were developed by our ancestors who relied exclusively on horseflesh for transportation, farm work and trade, racing enjoyment and military defense. This, then, is the chronicle of how our horse breeds were developed and why they remain an important part of our life today when an astonishing total of some six million horses in America alone reward owners of all ages and all interests.

Horses and children come in all sizes. These lucky youngsters are taking part in a 4-H horse show parade in Tucumcari, New Mexico.

The Arabian Horse

The land of the Nile, the Tigris and Euphrates has been called the cradle of civilization. If the influence of the ancient mid-eastern culture has been great in the development of other peoples, the influence of its prized horse strain has been just as important to the growth of later breeds. The horse that evolved from these eastern origins is the Arabian—the first true and actual breed to exist in equine history. His quality was so superior to anything the world had known that every future strain of light-weight riding horse was to seek the incorporation of Arab blood into its background. Even certain heavy horse types, as well as ponies, were to profit from crossings with Arabians. What the contemporary horse owes to the Arabian can only be imagined when we realize that about 80 per cent of all our modern breeds have, at one time or another, improved their lot by turning to this handsome, hardy little monarch of the desert. Never once has he failed to improve his fellow kind, for in centuries past, before other breeds were fully crystallized, it was a rule that any horse mated to an Arab produced offspring better than itself.

Of all those who profited from crossings with the Arab, it is probably the Thoroughbred who owes him the largest debt. Imported to England in the seventeenth and eighteenth centuries, the Darley Arabian, the Godolphin Barb and the Byerly Turk are the three eastern stallions which sired the families of Eclipse, Matchem and Herod, and it is this trio which in turn became the foundation sires of the entire Thoroughbred breed. For over 127 years, approximately 87 per cent of English Derby winners traced their lineage back to the Darley, while the other 13 per cent stemmed from the Godolphin and a lesser-known eastern sire called the Alcock Arabian. In fact, it is from the Alcock Arabian that gray Thoroughbreds of today inherit their color.

Even after the Thoroughbred was well established as a breed in its own right, it remained a practice for generations to mate Thoroughbred sires with Arab mares. In America, Arabians were registered in the Jockey Club along with Thoroughbred listings until as recently as 1943, clear evidence of the close association between the two strains.

The Standardbred also acknowledges a rich heritage of eastern blood early in its background, chiefly as a result of Imported Messenger who

13

was directly descended from the Darley Arabian. It was Messenger's great-grandson, Hambletonian 10, who became the foundation sire of the Standardbred breed and, as in the case of Thoroughbred stallions of that era, his abundant crop of foals was largely a result of crossings with Arab mares.

Even before the time of Columbus, the Spanish were astute judges of horseflesh, and through their experiences with the Moors knew that a horse from the east was a creature to be treasured. They took great pains to better their own stock by relying heavily on Arab blood, and consequently wherever the conquistadors landed—or were shipwrecked—they were accompanied by a well-bred gathering of horses of eastern descent which were to have an effect upon the future of the equine types in that region. It is fact that the American Quarter Horse, especially on the female side, may trace its earliest origins to the Arabian-blooded Spanish mounts brought ashore in Florida and Mexico. The desert influence was later reinforced by crossings between Quarter mares and Thoroughbred sires during early colonial breeding. And it is speculated that the ponies of Chincoteague—a small seaswept island off the coast of Maryland—are the descendants of Spanish horses who swam there to safety after a shipwreck. The ancient Spanish galleons prowling the waters of the British Isles may also account for the Arab blood known to have improved the wild pony strains of England, Ireland, Scotland and Wales.

For what reason is the Arabian to the modern horse very nearly what the biblical Adam was to man? What were his own origins and what qualities does she possess that have been so sought after by horsemen for centuries? It is precisely the answers to such questions that explain the continuing interest this glorious animal holds for his admirers.

Years ago the origins of the Arabian was the subject of controversy that found horsemen allying themselves with one of three different theories. Relatively recent archeological discoveries have helped to clear the air, but there are still some people who hold to a once-popular notion which most other experts now believe to be completely impossible. These people maintain that the Arabian's origins did not pre-date the birth of Christ, and that the strain was imported to Arabia—or neighboring regions —by such peoples as the Parthians, the Persians or the Scythians whose civilizations lasted from about 700 B.C. onward for several centuries. The main point of this argument is that the horse is a grazing animal and since Arabia is a desert he would never have migrated there on his own accord. A further claim is that because native Arab tribesmen were not themselves outstanding *riders*, they could not possibly have been so distinguished as breeders to come up with such an animal on their own.

Besides all other evidence, one fact disproves these beliefs—namely, fossil findings unearthed in Arabia indicate conclusively that in primitive ages the peninsula was not a desert. Pitted rocks testify to torrential rainfalls that encouraged lush vegetation. One section of lower Arabia called

Arabian filly yearlings at Friendship Farm, East Moline, Illinois. Note the classic Arabian features: dished face, short back, low withers, full barrel.

Arabian mares at Friendship Farm, Moline, Illinois. The deceptively small Arabian is fully capable of carrying a heavy stock saddle and a full-grown, heavy man.

the Nejd was not only fertile, abounding in grasses and foliage, but also had an underlayer of limestone which is precisely the subsoil element that exists in Kentucky and makes its bluegrass the best possible pasturage for horses. The Bible, to say nothing of numerous writings dating from more recent centuries, contains many references to "the forests of Arabia," and the Old Testament forewarns of the suns and winds, the warfare and famine that would eventually strip the land. Hence, we may be certain that at some point within the existence of early civilizations, regions of Arabia were indeed an ideal habitat for horses.

As to the superb horsemanship of the three northern civilizations, their excellence astride the horse does not award them the prize in the cultivation of the species. If there were a relationship between riding skills and breeding ingenuity, we would have to conclude that the finest horse strains of the present day were developed by such mounted athletes as the American Indian and the Russian Cossack. Yet, the fact is that neither of these peoples came anywhere near producing a breed of enduring quality.

Another rebuttal is, of course, the warring activities of the previously mentioned Hittites. Their early invasion of areas neighboring on Arabia pre-date Parthian, Persian and Scythian conquests by nearly 10 centuries, making these latter peoples seem like newcomers. It is possible that if imported horses drifted into the Arabian peninsula, they did so during the millennium that followed the Hittite invasion, and by the time the Scythians, Parthians and Persians came on the scene, the strain that might be traced to Hittite animals had already refined itself into the pure Arabian.

The legends and myths that seek to account for the origin of the breed provide a further case against the post-Christian theory. Although they cannot be interpreted as pure fact and, even worse, owe much of their local color to mistranslations, they nevertheless are so deeply rooted in Old Testament history that it is hard to believe that Arabian lore would take up this particular background if the beginnings of the horse were more recent. The folk-tale that reaches farthest back into biblical accounts contends that the breed arose from a wild mare received by Ishmael (2000 B.C.) as a divine gift from heaven. The mare was crippled as a result of being carried as a foal in a saddlebag on camelback, but nevertheless she bore a colt named *Benat El Ahwaj*—son of the crooked—and it is said that he became the sire of the first pure Arab strain called the Kuhaylan.

Thus the conclusion reached by most scholars is that by the time of Christ, the Arabian had already become a breed and was the backbone of such other oriental strains as the Barb (an Eastern type originally native to the Barbary Coast of Africa) and the Turk (similarly blooded and native to Turkey). Both the Barb and the Turk are simply larger and slightly coarser cousins of the Arab.

The only remaining arguments are between those people who feel that the breed had been native to Arabia since the evolution of the horse and flourished there in the wild, and those who feel that somewhere, far back in antiquity, adventurers imported horses which strayed into the peninsula and *then* became refined into a true wild strain. But most reliable historians feel that the Hittite invasion was the crucial step that brought the Arabian to his home.

To understand the magic the Arabian has for modern admirers it is first necessary to understand that the goals of today's Arabian breeders are completely different from those of horsemen involved in other strains. The Thoroughbred breeder and the breeders who specialize in the Standardbred, the Morgan, the Quarter Horse and so on, are constantly striving for improvement in their horse type and do not hesitate to modify the strain if necessary. Indeed, such horsemen are forever in search of some new genetic magic that will improve the special talents of their horses' offspring.

For the Arabian lovers, the improvement sought by other horsemen is something completely foreign to them. For this reason, the Arab has, in the minds of his critics, been left in the dust by progress. There is irony in the fact that after creating such breeds as the Thoroughbred, the American Saddle Horse and the Quarter Horse, the Arabian now plays second fiddle to them in speed, showiness and even, supposedly, in usefulness. But to appreciative owners of the breed, the Arabian, as he has existed for thousands of years, is a living work of art and one simply does not tamper with him. The breeder of the strain is, in a sense, the guardian of a trust— a timeless legacy which he is committed to preserve. He is not interested in betraying his cause to get a horse that can run a little bit faster, look a little bit fancier, or be slicker at jobs that didn't exist at the time the Arabian was formed.

For this reason the contemporary Arabian looks just as he did centuries ago. He is relatively small in size, averaging 15:2* at full growth, and is every inch a creature of beauty born of subtleties, not razzle-dazzle flashiness. His beauty is based on aristocratic fashioning of flesh and bone, a fragile-looking interplay of tendons and muscles and blood vessels in an animal that, in actuality, is anything but fragile.

The Arabian head looks as if it has been executed by the hand of a master sculptor. The bones are clear and refined, and have a delicacy unmatched in any other horse. Networks of vein are distinctly visible under the soft, taut skin. Sensitive ears curve into little lips that point toward each other when flickered to alertness, and at the velvety, dainty muzzle are wide, clear nostrils that expand freely when the horse is excited, revealing the pink inner surface. The two large discs of the cheeks are

---

* Fifteen hands and two inches. A hand is four inches; thus 15:2 equals 62 inches. Horses are measured from the ground to the top of the withers.

An Arabian competing in a costume class at Quentin, Pennsylvania, horse show.

Arabian yearlings at Friendship Farm, Moline, Illinois. Note the inward-pointing ears and the wide-set eyes.

smooth, rounded and so widely separated at the juncture of the throat that a baseball can fit into the hollow between them. The throat is completely unconstricted, meaning the entire length of the Arabian's respiratory apparatus is free from any obstruction that might interfere with his wind. It is this factor that permits him to be a great endurance horse and unequalled distance runner. The enormous, doe-like eyes of the Arab are boldly expressive and in a single gaze reveal his rare combinaton of great intelligence, sweetness of temperament, and fiery spirit. They are placed well apart from each other, noticeably lower down on the head as compared with other horses, and protrude distinctly outward from the face.

What most distinguishes the classic Arabian head from all others, however, is his profile. Seen from the side, his nose appears to "dish" inward but in fact the concavity is not caused so much by a depression along the nose but by a slight protrusion of the forehead. This wide and prominent forehead is known as the *jibbah* in Arabia and is valued among Bedouin tribesmen who maintain that the enlargement permits the horse to have a more sizeable brainpan and, therefore, greater intelligence. This is a theory that scientists have yet to confirm, for though it is true that the Arabian is endowed with excellent mental equipment, it is very likely that his superior intelligence and alert responses are a result of centuries of close association with his human masters.

The Arabian neck flows majestically out of strong, sloping shoulders into a subtle, elegant arch that merges with the head in a graceful union. This juncture of head and neck is another feature revered by the Bedouins who call this point the *mitbah*. Also characteristic of the Arab neck is the large, prominent windpipe vital to his superb lung power.

Along the barrel the Arab is extremely compact and sturdy to the degree that he is fully able to carry a 200-pound rider throughout a whole day's work. His withers are not notably prominent, but his ribs curve outward from a spine that is distinctly shorter than those of other horses. In fact, it is the shortness of the backbone which primarily accounts for its incredible supportive strength. While the ordinary horse has six lumbar or ribless vertebrae, 19 vertebrae that attach to ribs, and 18 tail vertebrae, the Arabian has but five lumbar vertebrae, 18—or often 17—vertebrae attaching to ribs, and 16 tail vertebrae. Nor is the back all that profits from the reduction in vertebrae. The tail, which on most other horses seems merely a decorative addition, is actually used as both rudder and brake and assists the Arab in stopping and turning.

The Arabian's underpinning is as deceptive as his small size, for the slender, delicate lines of his legs lead many horsemen to assume that these limbs cannot take much punishment. On the contrary, the bone of these slim extremities is as dense and smooth as ivory and far more durable than the more porous bonework of thicker-legged, more substantial-looking horses. They rarely stock up or bruise during shipping and are remarkably free from bone afflications.

Curiously enough, the Arab's legs are also often completely unmarked by the callosities (chestnuts or night-eyes) found along the inner surfaces of other horses' legs—or, if they do appear, they are so small as to be nearly undetectable. The absence of night-eyes, the unusual vertebrae count, and the fact that the teeth of the Arab are smaller and finer than any other type of horse's or pony's, are among the unique features that prompt some students of the horse to believe the Arabian should be classified as a species in his own right—Equus arabicus. (The late Lady Wentworth, a renowned English scholar, was a most articulate supporter of this theory.) The fact remains, however, that the Arab, as a physical specimen, is quite unlike any other horse, and that the best of his attributes are acquired in a harmonious blend by whatever breed should cross his path.

Under saddle the Arabian is a fiery little dynamo, yet left at leisure around the barnyard he is as docile and gentle as an overgrown lamb. It has already been noted that his intelligence is supreme in the equine world, and this is accompanied by an acute sense of loyalty. While the Bedouins connect these extraordinary virtues with the measure of the horse's brainpan, it is far more likely that they are more or less a hereditary result of the tender care the Arab has received for centuries at the hands of his Bedouin masters. While Arabian horsemen have never enjoyed a great reputation as riders, they are undoubtedly the most devoted and kindly owners of horses in the world.

To the Bedouin breeder, the birth of a foal is attended with far more ceremony and excitement than the birth of a child. He will know the animal's true ancestry by heart—clear back to the time of Mohammed, and may reconstruct a previous history, not altogether fictional, still farther back to the time of Christ. On this occasion he will take the pains to accurately and honestly document the horse's papers. And to the new arrival he will accord absolute freedom and loving hospitality. Foals and dams may wander at will around the camp, never tethered or coralled, and at night are welcomed into the master's tent to slumber beside the family. The young horse will not be indoctrinated to training, saddle or bridle until after the age of two, and often fully adult horses are given camel's milk instead of water as their liquid. If the animal is a mare, the Bedouin is even more painstaking, for in Arabia it is the mare, rather than the stallion, that is treasured for its breeding potential. Stallions are tolerated simply as a necessary part of the operation. It is his prize war mare that the sheik traditionally counts on to carry him into battle, and in their native country it is through the female line that the lineage of Arabian horses is traced. The traditional reverence attached to the Arabian mare in her homeland resulted at one time in strict protection of females born to the purest blood. Even as late as the last century it was like pulling hen's teeth to try to import an Arab mare of high quality out of the desert. Often those that were imported were released because they were thought to be sterile. Stallions however, were guarded less carefully.

Obviously a horse so treated and so prized is found to develop an alertness and attentive response to his human family. Small wonder, then, that the Arabian will arouse his Bedouin master at any inkling of danger, will gently awaken him at the break of day, and will run to his aid in any emergency. There are frequently repeated stories of Arab horses rescuing riders who have been wounded in battle and fallen to the ground. With a background such as this, it is not difficult to understand why the contemporary Arabian looks upon his human companions with kindliness.

But it is not the sweetness and light of his disposition that has made the Arab historically important to all other breeds, for most horsemen— of whatever era—do not place virtue ahead of performance. Nor can it be said in all truthfulness that Arabians were a source of extreme speed. The fact is that Arabians were swift only in proportion to their size and in relation to the horse types that existed centuries ago.

The vital quality the Arabian *did* contribute to his fellow kind was stamina. His endurance is something that surpasses all challenge, for when it comes to covering long distances, the Arab can run any other horse into the ground. Neither heat, nor treacherous terrain, nor the scantness of food and water can daunt him. There are persistent accounts of Arabians who have gone an incredible 400 miles in four consecutive days. Even this feat is topped by the endurance run of an Arab named Astraled who was ridden from Oregon to New Hampshire in 21 days, averaging 119 miles a day. The horse was 22 years old at the time of this accomplishment.

Until the last two or three decades, when the Arab was still relatively uncommon outside his native home, there had been a tendency for owners to treat him as something of an antique and to shy away from putting him to work or into competition with other horses. But now that there are some 25,000 registered Arabs in this country alone, and every indication that their popularity will increase still further, owners are at last proving that the Arab is as valuable a using horse as any other. He is entered in horse shows, ridden in the hunt field, and in the West, at such places as the Lazy V. V. Ranch in Colorado, flourishes under more rugged conditions and demonstrates that he is a first-rate working cow horse. His royal heritage, his historical influence, and his willing adaptation to the needs of modern horsemen make the Arab an animal that truly deserves a salute.

The Thoroughbred

"If you want a dog to race, you have to give him a rather silly look-ing mechanical hare to chase and keep him on a slim diet. Other animals have to be lured with a piece of meat suspended from a pole a couple of feet in front of their noses. But a horse will run just from the moral resolution to get somewhere ahead of his fellows."—ARTHUR VERNON, *The History and Romance of the Horse*

What in most horses is a "moral resolution to get somewhere ahead of his fellows" is, in the Thoroughbred, a compulsion. The Thoroughbred, quite simply, is born to run, to gather and thrust his long, fine limbs, propelling his lean, tall frame stride after stride with a speed that forbids all challenge by any other breed except the Quarter Horse, who is a pos-sible match only over short distances. At longer runs, from the half-mile upward, the Thoroughbred is not only the fastest of all horse types but considered by many naturalists to be the swiftest creature in the world. True, other animals, such as the cheetah, do achieve speeds which ap-proach 70 miles per hour. But this point of maximum acceleration is main-tained for only a fleeting moment, leaving the animal exhausted and limp after a few hundred yards, while the Thoroughbred, who runs at a credi-table 45 miles per hour or more, can easily continue his pace for a solid mile and more. Nor does he run because he is stimulated by either violence or hunger, as in the case of wild creatures. He runs because he wants to, because running is the fulfillment of his design as a being—and just be-cause he's a Thoroughbred, with a brand of courage and determination that will shrink neither in the face of pain nor death. No one among the older generation of horse lovers who recalls Humorist, the English racer who took many victories in the years that followed World War I, can ever erase from memory the triumph and agony surrounding his winning of the Epsom Derby crown. Less than three weeks after winning this grueling race, Humorist was found dead in his stall, lying in a pool of blood. Not until after an autopsy was performed was it revealed that throughout his racing career he had suffered from major pulmonary dis-orders and had won all of his races, including the Epsom Derby, virtually running on one lung.

24

Kentucky Derby winner Chateaugay, of Darby Dan Farms. Chateaugay's sire, Swaps, was also a Derby winner.

The famed Calumet Farm, Lexington, Kentucky.

In the span of one decade the illustrious Belmont Stakes has seen two great Thoroughbreds of this continent cross the finish line under similarly tragic circumstances. In 1958 Tim Tam bravely fought to second-place honors with a fractured sesamoid bone shattered into splinters, causing unbearable pain in his forefoot. And in 1967 the Canadian champion Cool Reception, challenging the winning Damascus for the lead, broke the vital cannon bone of his foreleg but pressed forward undaunted to arrive second at the wire.

These heroics are widely publicized and long remembered when performed by the greats who run in top stakes races, but they are no less common among unheralded campaigners who, despite their heart and spirit, just don't have the ability to make it to the big-time. Such a horse was Gallant Neb, a seasoned old racer who appeared in the field at Suffolk Downs in Massachusetts in what turned out to be his last race, nearly 30 years ago. Coming out of the far turn the pack got wedged into tight quarters and a collision took place. Gallant Neb went down flat on the track, but was not the kind of horse to stay there. He staggered to his feet and, running dead last and riderless, churned across the finish to the cheers of the crowd approving his game effort. As he wheeled past the stands the cheers turned to an awed hush and then a horrified gasp. His right rear leg was not only broken but virtually spinning loose from its joint. Yet not until after the wire was crossed did Gallant Neb finally relent and collapse pathetically to the track.

Of course there is among the strain, just as there are among other breeds, an occasional "no good bum" who'd rather dream of green pastures and warm sunshine than an appearance in the winner's circle. But in the Thoroughbred tribe such "dropouts" are exceedingly rare, for although few of them indeed can possess the physical talent of a Kelso, even the also-rans can be credited with giving the very last ounce of their gameness to the try. The elemental fact of the Thoroughbred is that by structure he is possessed of the look of eagles and by nature the heart of a lion.

The generosity of the Thoroughbred heart is a gift—in part divine and in part cultivated by man, who had the wisdom to selectively breed courageous horses to other stock of the same character, eventually producing an entire breed. Less mysterious than the quality of spirit is the quality of conformation, the "look of eagles" that makes it physically possible for one particular breed to achieve a speed that will leave any other horse in the dust. An obvious feature of the Thoroughbred build is the breed's extreme height. There are, to be sure, small members of the strain who barely make it to 15 hands but often the small racer can turn his compactness to advantage. With less body mass to control, he can develop an agility that will permit him to gather his energies more swiftly and make cleaner, faster breaks from the starting gate. Frequently, too, he can maneuver better than larger horses when the field closes into tight quarters, readily recovering his balance if jammed or bumped off

"The Thoroughbred will run just from the moral resolution to get somewhere ahead of his fellows."

stride. In general, however, the breed runs to an average height of roughly 16 hands and measurements of 17 hands and over are not uncommon. Among the light horse breeds, the American Saddle Horse family is the only other type which may grow to about the same size, but even here the Thoroughbred usually has the edge of an inch or two.

Unlike the Saddler, however, the Thoroughbred's tall frame stretches to a long horizontal distance so that the plane from head to tail measures to great extension. He presents an illusion of enormous horizontal reach, which is totally different from the restrained, compact attitude of the Saddler, who is his most nearly opposite kind. The body of the Thoroughbred is lean, angular and sloping, never round or chunky, even when fed to the plumper size that often comes with retirement. In fact, in the prime of racing condition, Thoroughbreds almost look thin and gaunt in comparison to other breeds. Toward the aft of the barrel they are noticeably wasp-waisted, tapered to a slender rear girth that seems all the smaller in view of their extreme depth through the heart—the huge area that runs from withers to lower chest just behind the forelegs. It is precisely this depth at the heart that is thought to endow the Thoroughbred with much of his stamina and running drive, and the fact that the size of the heart itself is bigger than that of much larger animals is significantly related to his courageous spirit.

To be maintained in proper racing condition Thoroughbreds are usually kept in a state where they have a constant nervous edge—a pent-up energy that explodes on the track. To keep this edge keen and fiery, race horses are rarely privileged to enjoy the friendly handling and working companionship with humans that makes the ordinary riding horse placid and wise to the disturbances of the world. The race horse is used to the sounds and sights involved in his trade—the clang of the starting gate, the rising roar of the crowd, the blare of a public address system—but his system is so highly geared that more ordinary disruptions like the playful romping of a dog, the whine of a motorcycle, the fluttering of laundry hanging on a clothesline are apt to send him into fits of fear simply because he is not regularly exposed to everyday activities. When not being shipped to and from the track, working out in the tranquil dawn, or actually performing before the crowd, he lives a pleasant but rather secluded life. Thus, when faced with strange objects and situations he reacts with a flightiness that would seem perfectly silly in any other horse and appears to contradict his other instincts which are so valiant. Such skittishness often gives rise to the opinion that Thoroughbreds, despite their athletic glory, are not really very bright. This, of course, is untrue. Race horses are simply a product of their environment and close in-breeding which is hardly conducive to developing a docile, even-tempered disposition. Even so, many of them are remarkably easy-going and kind, and it is certain that most of them would be more so if treated to a relaxed and sociable association with man. When given an opportunity to be friendly, they often develop close affections for people and a variety of barnyard pets including dogs, cats, chickens, pigeons, goats, donkeys, cows and sheep. Indeed, far from being dim-witted, the Thoroughbred has an alert mind. He has had, of course, little experience in the wild as a free wanderer forced to see to his own needs, and thus he is not shrewd, or blessed with an intuition of what's best for his own survival. On the contrary, he will run until he drops in his tracks rather than cleverly take advantage of a chance for rest. This, however, is a result of his generosity rather than stupidity, for the Thoroughbred is endowed with a very obvious intelligence which, while not usually "foxy" in character, is inquiring and sensitive. The very look of his head will reflect these qualities. Although the Thoroughbred head is not quite as small and dainty as the Arabian's, it is nevertheless delicate in proportion to the rest of his body, and refined and clean. His muzzle, like the Arab's, tapers off to small, gentle, velvety nostrils that expand freely with speed or excitement, showing the hot pink of blood vessels inside. His ears are petite and frequently, like his Arabian ancestors', point inward at the tips. His eyes are round and bold with a bright, wide-set look, and his nose may either be perfectly straight or have the suggestion of an inward dish that is also reminiscent of the Arabian. His skin is tight, sensitive and thin, revealing the veins beneath and the sinewy sculpture of muscling which, as in any athlete, is long and flat.

Of all the Thoroughbred's characteristics perhaps the most unique is his extreme legginess. His limbs are lithe, slender, finely structured and very long. Once propelled into action they move with low, pendulous, earth-eating strides that may, as in the case of the great Man O' War, cover no less than 25 feet in one sequence. To achieve this fantastic horizontal reach, his action is always free, loose and flexible, and implementing the forward thrust of each gigantic cycle is the line from point of hip to hock, often referred to as the "drive shaft." The Thoroughbred's "drive shaft" is as a rule longer than that of other horses and is thought to be a crucial source of his running power.

The long, slender legs of the Thoroughbred that enable him to cover ground truly by leaps and bounds are also his most vulnerable points. Indeed, the ease of their injury under contemporary racing conditions has given rise to the opinion that the Thoroughbred is a fragile-limbed animal —and certainly the number of cases of lameness, early breakdowns and premature retirement due to leg and foot ailments would seem to support this conclusion. But if one looks beyond the statistics and comes to grips with the reason for these casualties, there emerges a very good argument against charges of frailty. The blame, instead of falling on the horse, should be on the overwhelming financial pressures involved in modern racing. The sport has expanded to such an extent that it has achieved the rank of big business with huge investments needed to operate the huge modern racing tracks. But the burden of the pressure and the pinch of rising

Thoroughbred mare and foals, Lexington, Kentucky.

costs is felt most by owners and trainers who have sunk fortunes and their professional reputations into the breeding and grooming of top-scale racers. Though it would appear that the purses are generous, providing ample reward for these efforts, the sad reality is that even the six-figured prizes are but a drop in the bucket compared to the expenditures connected with getting a decent string of horses from the breeding farm to the post. Anxious to regain at least some of this huge investment, owners and trainers have no choice but to run entries at the earliest possible date, which is when their horses are fledglings of two years old.

Meantime, the two-year-old Thoroughbred has just started to really develop. Like the awkward, gangly adolescent, the race horse seems to go on growing forever, and at two years of age may have achieved most of his size but has only begun to acquire his substance. His bones do not finally become hardened and set until he is four to five years old, and the earlier the horse is raced before that age, the more severe will be the crushing, pounding strain of running at all-out sped—a strain that is punishing to even the fully developed animal. Yet what owner in this expensive age can afford to bide his time for four years before even being able to separate the wheat from the chaff in his stable? And how can one hold up to criticism the normal desire to get a reasonably prompt return to offset the mounting outlay of funds? One can only hope for an eventual solution to the problem and lament its unfortunate side effects—the many cases of lameness and breakdown in young horses and the sudden appearance of less than first-rate racers scrambling for all available prizes. But above all it should be recognized that the fault is not the Thoroughbred's, for given a chance to complete his growth he is as sound and solid as any other horse.

No better evidence of the Thoroughbred's substance exists than his brilliant performance as a steeplechaser, hunt racer, and practical hunting mount in the field. The colorful and historic sport of hunting, now a highly popular diversion of horse owners in many parts of the country, presents a combination of speed, rigid obstacles and terrain that is sometimes frozen solid—a combination that automatically eliminates the unsound or fragile horse from all hope of participation. Admittedly, during the course of the chase the hunter does not have to contend with the stopwatch. The pace will be broken with pauses as the hounds halt to check the scent, with leisurely canters as the pack steadfastly finds and follows the trail, and then with headlong, blinding gallops over rugged country as the quarry is finally sighted and cries of "Gone Away!" and "Tally Ho!" ring through the crisp, chill air. Up and down hill, through and around dense thickets, among winding, wooded trails the field will then charge at full speed to leap hurdles of solid timber, brick and stone, water, brush, and even iron. A sharp slam against these objects or an awkward jump, throwing the horse off balance, would spell certain doom for the overly delicate horse long before friend Charley Fox was at last run to his grave; but

The Thoroughbred, "the athlete of the horse world," makes a splendid mount for the rugged, hard-riding game of polo.

whenever the pace is hot and the distance long, the man on the Thorough-bred will be in front. And the reason he is there is that, instead of being pressured into riding young horses inadequately developed for the strain, the hunting man can use the mature and seasoned mount who is doubtless a few seconds slower in time but hardier and more durable.

There are subtle but recognizable differences in the conformation of the hunting Thoroughbred compared to his racing brothers—differences that arise from the nature of hunting in the field and running on the track. The hunter is not obliged to shave seconds off the clock, but he must have, instead, the thrusting, vaulting power to handle steep and sometimes treacherous hurdles, the rugged substance to tolerate a stiff rap on the legs should he misjudge his fence, and the resources to stay with the pack for a distance of 30 or 40 miles over a period of some four or five exhausting hours. Hence the hunter is usually not only older and more fully developed than the racer, but is rarely as lean, slender and finely honed. Rather, he is conditioned to fuller, heavier proportions—a bold, solid, more massive size with thicker, more rounded muscling to give him the vertical propulsion over jumps. This is not to say that he does not still conform to the rangy, extended look that stamps the Thoroughbred, but merely that within this framework he has a weightier, stauncher build.

The steeplechase horse, who races over hurdles at regular pari-mutuel tracks, and the hunt-racer, who runs at semi-private meets over long (often four-mile) courses with death-defying jumps to simulate real hunting con-ditons, are a miraculous combination of the mighty flat racer and the solid Thoroughbred hunter. In conformation, these racing jumpers are a subtle blend of the features of both these types. Like the flat runner, they are uncommonly lithe without an extra ounce of fat to be found on their frame, but like the hunting mount, their quarters have an ever-so-slightly rounder, heavier muscling to give them the necessary jumping lift. Here again the winners in these races are often over five years old. Any suspicion of leg weakness in the Thoroughbred can be dispelled when we realize that speed so multiplies the force of impact on landing after a jump that the strain for the hunt racer carrying 140 pounds in the saddle is greater than that of a hunter carrying over 200 pounds and taking the same fence at a more moderate pace. Since the jumper usually first lands on a single forefoot only, one shudders to imagine the overwhelming force of this impact.

The recorded history of the Thoroughbred is officially acknowledged to be approximately 260 years long and technically commences in the waning years of the seventeenth century and early years of the eighteenth. It was in 1691 that a British Army officer named Captain Byerly brought to England a horse acquired in Turkey—a horse destined to become known as the Byerly Turk. In 1704 Thomas Darley purchased in Syria and im-ported to the island another oriental stallion who was the single horse destined to have the greatest influence on the development of the new breed. This was the Darley Arabian. Some years later the third great

The start of the parade to the post at Saratoga.

Nothing is too rough for the Thoroughbred. Here a "timber" horse takes a jump in the Virginia Gold Cup point-to-point race.

oriental sire appeared—the Godolphin Barb, owned by Lord Godolphin and thought to have come from the Barbary Coast of Africa. From these three desert stallions descend the only three male stirps (or lines of descent) which endure to this day in direct line from father to son to form the Thoroughbred dynasty. The three founding fathers are: Matchem, foaled in 1758, a grandson of the Godolphin; Herod, in 1758, a great-great-grandson of the Byerly Turk; and Eclipse, in 1764, a great-great-grandson of the Darley Arabian. Within one century after the birth of these titans, the fastest breed of horse the world has ever known would come to be firmly established.

The vital role of Arab blood in the cultivation of the Thoroughbred horse is shown in the close relationship between the Darley, the Godolphin and the Byerly and the unique offspring traced to their bloodlines. And yet it is folly to believe that they are the sole and exclusive basis for the Thoroughbred. The Thoroughbred has existed for 260 years, but the Arabian has existed twenty times as long and it seems naïve to imagine that during those centuries no other Arabian horses touched on English shores to mate with the larger, cold-blooded stock native to northern Europe. The case, in fact, was quite the reverse, for European horsemen, notably the Spanish, had recognized centuries earlier the value of oriental blood in refining and improving their own animals. Through exchanges, both military and commercial, horses of notable desert extraction were sought and secured for precisely these purposes. England's Charles II, often called "the father of the British turf," actively sought to build up his light cavalry in 1660 by importing ever-increasing numbers of Barbs, Turks and Arabs. He re-established the Royal Stud, complemented it with his collection of Royal Mares, took over the racecourse at Newmarket where he himself actively participated in the races, and made Newmarket the hub of British racing, which it has remained to this day.

The effect of Charles' importations and the similar breeding energies of many horsemen generations before his time was to produce a variety of English hybrid horse, part oriental and part cold-blooded, which was tall, and probably fairly leggy and fast compared to other types of the period. The evolution of this British hybrid type must be considered a crucial factor in the origin of the Thoroughbred; otherwise there is no satisfactory explanation for the difference in size and speed of horses that were later developed. When the ultimate union took place between a high caliber of hybrid mare and top stallions of eastern blood, the outcome was offspring that were much faster than either parent, and faster than the produce of either parent when mated back to the parent's own kind. The origins of the Thoroughbred, therefore, are not the result of a sudden, magical transformation, but of a planned improvement of an existing British running horse which worked to superb effect when mares were mated with pure desert stallions of the best quality.

The effect of the Thoroughbred on the English sporting scene of the 1700's, plus the wholehearted support of Queen Anne, who founded the Ascot races, led to the organization of the British Jockey Club in 1750 and the appearance of the first accurate registry of pedigrees, the General Stud Book. During the rule of Queen Anne and the succeeding Georges, fox hunting began to prosper as a swift and lively sporting pageant owing to the speed and ease with which the Thoroughbred negotiated the terrain's obstacles. No longer did the hunting field meander and dawdle in outings that formerly were more social affairs than sport. The Thoroughbred increased the pace and heightened the spirit of the chase. The approach of the Industrial Revolution increased hunting's popularity by producing a flourishing middle class to participate in it in great numbers. Meanwhile, the same jumping facility that caused the Thoroughbred to envigorate hunting acted to promote steeplechasing—racing from point to point under simulated hunt conditions. The English enthusiasm for both these sports was matched in the New World, where the first pack of hounds arrived in Maryland in 1650.

At its outset, flat racing in America was conducted under informal, folksy —and often rather unruly—circumstances. Most of the events were match races between two horses, and the crowds in attendance were feisty when it came to rooting for their favorite. Close finishes were usually settled by a free-for-all or in a court of law. As to the contests themselves, the dense forests in the colonies at first prevented distance racing. There simply was not enough cleared land to provide suitable courses. Instead, match races were held on the main streets of villages or a brief stretch of road cleared for the occasion. Horses performing in the races were specially bred for these short distances. They were animals that blasted like a bolt of lightning over a quarter-mile dash and were, as well, hardy, serviceable workers at the many domestic tasks involved in community life. In time colonial horsemen refined this type into an altogether remarkable strain that filled the dual role of short distance racer and everyday "using" horse—the Famous and Celebrated American Quarter Pather, now known as the Quarter Horse.

However, as colonial life became more civilized, larger tracts of land were cleared, and as commerce and trade enlarged, the importation of blooded horses from England increased. The first arrival was Bulle Rocke, a son of the Darley Arabian, shipped to America in 1730. Once its roots were established, Thoroughbred breeding was destined to expand in this country, and the construction of oval tracks made end-to-end Thoroughbred distance racing possible and attractive. The Quarter Horse, in the process, migrated west with the ever-adventurous frontier settlers.

During the Revolutionary War, racing existed largely for the diversion of British soldiers while native stock suffered considerable depletion as horses were recruited to supply the Continental Army's cavalry. But when the war ended, new infusions of blood came once again from England, including a prominent small gray stallion named Medley. He was followed by Shark, then Messenger, and finally Diomed. Messenger had a profound influence on Thoroughbred breeding and also sired offspring who played a crucial role in the origins of the Standardbred and Saddle Horse. A recent Thoroughbred descendant of Messenger is the immortal Kelso who retired in 1967 with record winnings of nearly $2,000,000.

Diomed, who achieved renown with his Epsom Derby victory, sired Sir Archy, the first important native-bred American stallion, and in so doing became a patriarch of the American Turf, much as Eclipse was to the British turf. Other early descendants of Diomed were his grandchildren, American Eclipse and Haynie's Maria, who was General Andrew Jackson's nemesis. After 13 consecutive defeats of the Jackson stable, besting Maria became an obsession with the general. Doubtless he went to his grave a sadder man that his ambition was never satisfied.

Racing's popularity flourished during the period between the Revolutionary and Civil Wars, yet the shadow of ill-feeling between the states was beginning to loom a shade darker. Hostilities erupted in 1842 during the famous race between Boston, a great runner from Virginia, and the Northern-owned mare, Fashion. A surly mob of what some reports estimate to have been 100,000 spectators overran Long Island's Union Race Course, crowding onto the track itself, barely leaving room for the contestants. Fashion ran to an unexpected triumph that is commemorated in New York with Aqueduct's annual Fashion Stakes.

As it turned out, Fashion proved to be only an average brood-mare, but Boston sired the runner Lexington, who defeated his sibling Lecomte in the Great State Post Stake in New Orleans in 1854 and went on to become one of the great sires of the American turf.

Lest the quality and substance of our early Thoroughbred be doubted, it should be pointed out that it was frequently the custom in those days to judge contests on the basis of the best of three four-mile heats, thus requiring the entries to run a total of 12 miles before the outcome of a single race was decided. The English had long since abandoned the grueling heat system in favor of more exciting single runs. This practice was gaining popularity here, only to have the entire breeding establishment in the Southeast wiped out and the sport completely disrupted by the Civil War. Fortunately, while plants in the Kentucky bluegrass region suffered severe ravages, they were spared the worst of the devastation and survived to become the center of Thoroughbred breeding after the war. The rest of the impoverished South, once a bastion of breeding and racing, was to acquire a Post-Civil War morality which frowned upon the sport and caused it to wither in all its strongholds save Louisiana and Maryland. And New England, formerly the seat of strait-laced Puritanism, began to view the sport with a Post-Civil War open-mindedness. (Today racing prospers in all New England states except Connecticut.)

During this period New York and Maryland received special stimulus with the opening of such historic tracks as Saratoga in 1864 where in that year the Travers Stakes was inaugurated; and Pimlico, near Baltimore, in

1870, where the Preakness Stakes is traditionally run as the second of the Triple Crown events. The Belmont Stakes, named in honor of August Belmont who was one of racing's most aristocratic enthusiasts of the time, is the climax of the Triple Crown contests. Established in 1867, it remains New York's most celebrated race. A few years later, in 1875, Churchill Downs opened in Kentucky and with it came the founding of the Kentucky Derby, which is now first in the sequence of the Triple Crown series. Hereafter American racing was to enter its memorable "Golden Age."

In this glorious era between the end of the Civil War and the beginning of the twentieth century emerged many of the greatest names in racing: Ruthless, winner of the inaugural Nursery and Belmont Stakes, as well as the Travers; undefeated Norfolk; Kentucky, Longfellow and Henry Bassett; Hindoo, Domino and Ben Brush—all champions who improved the American Thoroughbred stock by the brilliance of their progeny. But the greatest stud of them all was Lexington, son of Boston and sire of horses who won three of the first five Travers and nine of the first 15 Belmont Stakes. Not even sires like Hanover, Broomstick, Bull Lea and Nasrullah ever approached Lexington's record.

The unforgettable horses in the decades immediately prior to World War II cannot be measured by the same standards used in considering the horses of previous ages because, as the twentieth century progressed, conditions of racing became drastically different. Four-mile races no longer existed, causing a simultaneous shift that now emphasized extreme speed rather than extreme stamina. Tracks became faster as a result of more scrupulous maintenance and a more scientific approach to their construction. Thus, in all fairness, it is impossible to evaluate the twentieth-century crop of runners, which have raced under the most advantageous circumstances, as compared with their nineteenth-century relatives. All that is certain is that among the pre-World War II champions, all comparisons begin and end with Man O' War and Exterminator. Man O' War, who lost but one decision, and that as a result of just bad racing luck, retired to become one of the most important modern sires in America. Exterminator, so lean he was nicknamed the "galloping hatrack," had a spectacular eight-year career which included 100 races, of which he won 50 and was unplaced in but 16. He was a true stayer, without flaw, who could win at six furlongs or at two miles and always under top weight. Their careers overlapped, and a hypothetical race between them has to this day remained a subject for hot debate. Other amazing horses of an over-all quality that was not to be matched were: Equipoise, the epitome of the Thoroughbred—perfection in conformation, disposition, and performance—who unfortunately was plagued by a bad foot which all but canceled out a brilliant three-year campaign, primarily in the handicap division; Regret, the only filly ever to win the Kentucky Derby; Zev, who won international recognition for American racing by beating the British Derby winner, Papyrus, in a special match race; Gallant Fox, the only Triple Crown winner in history to have a son, Omaha, share that honor with

Thoroughbred brood-mares and foals, in the heart of the bluegrass country in Kentucky. (Photo by Dept. of Public Information, Kentucky)

him. Then there was the golden-coated Discovery, who earned the reputation of being one of the greatest weight carriers in our turf history. Some stables with top horses will not permit their horses to start if more than 130 pounds is allotted them, yet Discovery shouldered 143 pounds. At stud he proved to be a great brood-mare sire and counts Native Dancer among his offspring. Then there was Triple Crown winner, War Admiral, who came from one of the last crop of Man O' War foals.

World War II brought a temporary lull to racing, but did produce two Triple Crown winners: Whirlaway, in 1943, and Count Fleet. Whirlaway was a crowd-pleasing horse with an electrifying style, for he liked to drop off the pace and then make a stretch run that was unbelieveable. The immediate postwar years, 1946 and 1948, produced two more Triple Crown champions: Assault, who proved to be sterile after retirement, and Citation, sired by Bull Lea. There has been no Triple Crown winner since.

Among the recent generation of racers, one of the most sensational was Native Dancer, with a 25 foot stride equal to Man O' War's. Unfortunately, an injury forced his retirement when he was undisputed champion. Other postwar greats have been Swaps, Round Table, Nashua, Stymie and Tom Fool, and finally, Kelso—winner five consecutive times of the Jockey Gold Cup, elected five consecutive times to the title of Horse of the Year, and holder of the world's all-time record for track money earnings. Kelso, indeed, is a horse of a lifetime, one who, at a time when racing is often regarded as a cold, calculated business, has symbolized all the qualities of heart and *noblesse* that make the Thoroughbred a prince among horses. He raced to standing ovations and tears of joy shed by usually unmovable veteran track goers. In motion he was a vision of physical splendor, yet all the time you watched him run you knew that what the late Sunny Jim Fitzsimmons, trainer of champions, had said was true. When it comes to Thoroughbreds, "It's the part you can't see that matters."

The Quarter Horse

The much quoted definition of the American Quarter Horse as a "sleepy little critter than can unwind like lightnin'" sums up the remarkable characteristics of America's largest registered breed of horses. The word "sleepy" can be interpreted as describing the Quarter Horse's docility and general good nature. He is "little" in the sense that he is nearly always shorter than his rangier Thoroughbred cousin (though his compact, well-muscled body may weigh up to 300 or so pounds more). And anyone who has seen a top cattle-cutting or racing Quarter Horse in action knows that, with his powerful physique and deceptive alertness, he can indeed "take off" like a bolt from the blue.

Where did this outstanding equine performer come from, and how did he acquire the outstanding qualities that have made him so popular? His is a story that traces back to the earliest periods in the European colonization of North America.

The horses that came from the Old World to the New were from two principal sources. Those that arrived in the West and far South came from Spain, while those which were landed in the East came from Great Britain. The American Quarter Horse inheritance is from both of these origins. And this was a fusion of blood that took place beginning at a very early stage in his development. For while the modern-day evolution of the breed has been greatly influenced by the inbreeding of good "blooded" stock—strains of pure or almost Thoroughbred derivation—upon the better grade of Spanish-descended mares found in the American Southwest, a similar type of cross had already taken place many years before in colonial Virginia and the Carolinas. This happened when the British settlers bred the imported blood stock from England with the tough little Chickasaw horses which the Indians had stolen from the Spanish. Some of these horses might have come from Florida, but the better grade seem to have been originally taken from Spanish haciendas far to the west and to have been passed eastward, tribe by tribe, until they entered the Piedmont uplands. Some of these, the British found running in a wild, or "feral," state. But they obtained most of them by barter with the Indians:

The Quarter Horse takes his name from his great reputation for speed at the quarter-mile distance. This so-called sport of "quarter pathing" was an extremely popular pastime of the early colonists of Tidewater Maryland and Virginia and, a little later, of the Carolinas. There is also evidence that the sport flourished in Pennsylvania, New Jersey, on Long Island in New York, and even in New England.

Most of the countryside along the eastern seaboard in pre-Revolutionary America was heavily forested. The English, however, had brought with them a centuries-old love of horse racing, and the only practical way in which they could continue the sport was to conduct their race meets on short straightaways. The very earliest of these contests were held on the streets of the young settlements. (To this day, many of these communities have thoroughfares called "Race Street.") This practice being dangerous to the citizenry, they were obliged to hack race paths from a quarter of a mile to 500 yards in length out of the bush.

The horse which the colonists had evolved from the cross of the English "blood" on the Chickasaws proved ideal for this kind of "short" racing. One visitor to the Virginia plantation country wrote: "I am confident that there is not a horse in England . . . that can excel them for rapid speed, and [they] likewise make an excellent saddle horse for the road." This latter observation is worthy of note since in the early seventeenth century there were few settlers who could afford to keep horses just for racing. The horse that competed in these Quarter meetings had also to carry his master on his daily rounds, and he was often hitched to a wagon or plow as well. Thus, from the very outset, versatility, a quality that is still one of his outstanding characteristics, became a part of the Quarter Horse's heritage.

Hardiness was another. Usually underfed and overworked, these horses were in most cases turned out into the woods for the night, even in freezing weather, to forage for themselves. Thus did the Quarter Horse, through a "survival of the fittest" process, become toughened to harsh living conditions. His great adaptability in this respect has marked the breed throughout its history.

Toward the close of the seventeenth century, the lowland plantations began to grow larger due to the huge profits they were reaping from tobacco, now greatly in vogue in England and on the continent. And, as more and more land was cleared, the old-time sport of Quarter racing began to give way to the "end-to-end" distance racing that was practiced in the old country. For some decades before the American Revolution, the type of horses which a century later would be officially designated "Thoroughbreds" were being imported from Britain to participate in three- and four-mile races that were becoming popular.

Meanwhile, Quarter Horses and Quarter racing were pushed inland, ever westward. After the Revolution, they would accompany the pioneers through Kentucky and Tennessee, up into Ohio and Michigan, and eventually down into the great Southwest, as the frontier of the new republic rolled toward the Pacific Ocean.

It was some 20 years before the colonies proclaimed their independence,

With the increase in the horse population, trail riding is a fast-growing sport. Here are some of the participants in the annual trail ride sponsored by the Ohio Quarter Horse Association, Rio Grande, Ohio. (American Quarter Horse Association)

The Quarter Horse is endowed with "cow savvy" which is the result of selective breeding over the course of centuries. (Courtesy The Cattleman)

though, that a stallion of the fashionable "distance" type was brought into Virginia by a well-to-do planter and shipper named Mordecai Booth. This horse was Janus, an animal who had compiled a superior racing record in England but who had gone lame and been retired to stud. In Virginia, Janus recovered his soundness and again found his way to the winner's circle.

Janus is described as having, from the shoulders back, the finest conformation of any horse then seen in the colonies. Though small—less than 15 hands—he had endless racing stamina, or "bottom," which, when he was crossed to mares of the blood, he was able to transmit with great success to his descendants.

At the time Janus arrived in Tidewater Virginia, Quarter racing had not wholly passed from the scene. And it is apparent that some experimental breeding of Janus to Quarter-type mares established the fact that when crossed upon this sort of stock, his blood, through some quirk of genetics, engendered blinding speed. This was in precise contrast to the great distance he built into his progeny on the blood horse side of the fence.

There is, perhaps, a very valid explanation for this breeding peculiarity. The scholar of bloodlines, John O'Connor, has pointed out that this good "nick" between Janus and the Chickasaw-Spanish mares was not necessarily an accident. Janus, he noted, was a grandson of the Godolphin Barb. The origin of most Spanish horses was also the Barbary Coast of Africa. Their ancestors were brought from that part of the world into Spain over a period of many centuries during the Moorish occupation. The great success that Janus enjoyed with the Spanish-descended mares, O'Connor says, could well be attributed to the breeding law of "like breeds like."

Whatever the reason, the fact was so well proven that Janus was dispatched on a long tour of stud duty in "southside" Virginia and North Carolina where Quarter racing was still very much the rage. And, while the Quarter-type race horse was indeed already well-established, Janus' prepotency as a Quarter stallion was so great that he appears in the direct line of descendancy of nine of the 11 original Quarter Horse families, as set down in the stud book of the American Quarter Horse Association.

It is true that the Spanish conquistadors who settled Mexico and the American Southwest were experienced stock men. The horses they brought with them had in their breeding backgrounds countless generations of selective mating to produce "cow savvy" and handling ease. In fact, much of the lingo of our own western horsemanship is derived from the Spanish: "lariat," for example, from the Spanish "la reata"; "hackamore," from "jaquima"; even "buckaroo," comes from the Spanish "vaquero," meaning cowboy. There is no doubt that early American cattlemen in the Southwest learned much of their know-how from the Spanish-descended "rancheros" who settled this part of the country, and they bred their horses to the best of the Spanish stock to produce their finest cow ponies.

Yet it is a fact that neither American cattle-ranching nor American cow ponies originated on the great Western plains. Both had their beginnings

The amazing versatility of the Quarter Horse and his ability to work closely with man and with other horses makes him the undisputed star of the rodeo circuit. The events pictured here are calf roping (left), cutting (lower left), team roping (right and lower right).

The favorite sport of Quarter Horse enthusiasts, particularly girls, is barrel racing.

way back east, in early colonial times. As long ago as 1710, more than a half century before our Independence was declared, stock men in South Carolina and Georgia had already devised the cattle pen—the corral with its wide funnel-like mouth—into which the cattle were worked by mounted cowboys, cracking bull whips and shooting off firearms, just as they would do nearly two centuries later on the prairies of Texas.

To aid them in this work, no horse was found that could match the tireless and agile Quarter Horse, with his endless capacity for hardship and slim rations. And when these eastern cow ponies—with their already strong tincture of Spanish Chickasaw-Barb blood—were eventually mated with the Barb-types brought in by the Spanish, the result was the best mount for cattle work that had ever been seen.

The Quarter Horse Stud Book shows that, after the family established in 1832 by the Thoroughbred Copperbottom, the breed had to get along for a lengthy span of years without much breeding help from the blood horse, at least of the pure Thoroughbred. As a matter of fact, of the 13 foundation sires which the Quarter Horse Association has added since Copperbottom, there is not officially one Thoroughbred among them (with the possible exception of the twentieth-century stallion Peter McCue, over whose breeding a controversy has swirled for a score of years). Today, Quarter Horse breeders have mixed in liberal dosages, particularly in the breeding of horses for racing purposes. But during the long interim period between Copperbottom and the establishment of the Quarter Horse Registry and Stud Book, barely a quarter-century ago, a number of breeding influences had varying impact on the background of the modern horse.

In various parts of the Southwest, most notably in Oklahoma, Standardbred stallions were crossed on Quarter mares. Some breeders, like Captain King and the Klebergs who succeeded him at the famous King Ranch in Texas, were among the few financially able to employ Thoroughbred studs. But they too experimented, from time to time, with Standardbreds, Morgans, Arabians, and American Saddle Horses in their search for the best possible stock horse. (How successful King Ranch eventually became at producing this kind of animal was recognized when the Quarter Horse Association honored that establishment by awarding the number 1 to the King Ranch's Wimpy, when the first Registry appeared.)

Of the 13 stallions of later date which were finally admitted to the Stud Book as founders of families, the two names which are probably the most encrusted with lore and legend are those of Steel Dust and Traveler.

Steel Dust's prowess in the stud was such that, for years, horses of the type we now recognize as Quarter Horses were actually called "Steeldusts." In fact, so mighty was his reputation as a good foal getter, that there was a widespread counterfeiting of pedigrees to work in the magic name of "Steel Dust." This reached such a degree that, as Phil Stong commented, "there was not a saddled maverick under a cowhand that was not a Steeldust or you fought the owner."

Steel Dust was originally acquired in Illinois and was brought, sometime in the 1840's, to the Lancaster, Texas, ranch of Middleton Perry. He was a fantastically fast runner and was able to communicate this quality with great reliability to his heirs—the real ones, anyway.

Even more amazing was the career of Traveler, which was a sort of rags-to-riches saga in the world of Western equines. When we first meet Traveler, he is pulling a road grader on the Texas Pacific Railroad line. The rumor is that the contractor who owns him, won him in a crap game. Now he passes into the hands of a character named Triggerfoot Self, in exchange for a mule. Triggerfoot takes Traveler to his farm in Baird, Texas. He is, by all accounts, a pretty old horse at this time but apparently he has never been saddled, nor does he relish this idea at all. When Traveler finally gets used to a rider, Triggerfoot notices he has speed that is nothing short of fantastic. Soon Traveler trounces all the best Quarter racers around Callahan County. Triggerfoot sells him at a tidy profit to Brown Seay, one of the leading Quarter Horse racing men in the state in whose keep he continues his winning ways against the finest horses in Texas. He retires without ever suffering defeat.

No one has ever cast any doubt on Traveler's racing ability. But the great success he subsequently enjoyed in the stud has been credited, by some, to the fine mares to which he was bred. His defenders, on the other hand, point out that he got two of his fastest racers and a son who went east where he became the top polo pony of his day, all out of a rickety old mare who shambled around Baird pulling an ice wagon.

Though the Quarter Horse had journeyed far to get to Texas, and would travel farther still—to the Far West and most recently to England, Australia and New Zealand—the Lone Star State can be called the real cradle of the modern Quarter Horse. Here, more than in any other locale, was evolved the kind and hardy animal who, at handling livestock, knows no peer, and who can blitz down a short race course faster than any other breed of horse.

Physically, the Quarter Horse is admirably put together for both these purposes. (It is true that there are marked differences in conformation between the stock and the racing types, the latter often reflecting a heavier infusion of Thoroughbred blood in its slimmer legs and longer, flatter muscles. Nevertheless, even the racing Quarter Horse must pass rigid examination for Quarter Horse conformation in order to be eligible to compete, and it is quite astonishing how these speedsters will retain that distinctive conformation despite repeated inter-breeding with Thoroughbreds.)

The good looks of the Quarter Horse—and at his best he is one of the best-looking of all breeds—are the byproduct of his great usefulness and bespeak his suitability for the work he does so well.

The first thing that strikes the observer is the remarkable balance in his stance. He stands—and moves—with his legs well beneath him, legs

Quarter Horse racing is the fastest-growing sport in the U.S. With his powerful hindquarters and short stride, the Quarter Horse eats up the ground as he blazes down the straightaway. Here is the finish of The Inaugural at Ruidoso Downs, New Mexico.

which are characterized by smooth joints and very short cannons. This poise, coupled with his extremely alert responses, is what enables the Quarter Horse to dart forward to either side or to back up with incredible agility. In all these movements, however sudden or extreme, he never seems clumsy or awkward but always light on his feet, moving with grace and rhythm.

The beholder's eye is also drawn to the very distinctive head of the good Quarter Horse. It is short and broad. The eyes are set well apart, reflecting both kindness and intelligence. The ears are unusually small and pointed. The muzzle is short and the jaws unusually well-developed.

His top line is distinguished by a full neck, slightly arched at the crest, descending into a deep, broad chest. The withers are of medium height but well-sharpened to accept the saddle. His back is short and the hindquarters are broad and heavy and very powerfully muscled. It is from this power plant that he produces his great drive.

For generations, the cattlemen had been breeding selectively to produce a horse of just this type, not so that he could win ribbons in halter classes, but to do the specific job of handling cattle. The sum total of the Quarter Horse's physical and mental attributes bear eloquent testimony that these men knew what they were doing. But for many years, no particular effort was directed toward establishing a central registry and stud book. The larger and more meticulous cattle operations and many individual horse breeders, in many instances, kept private breeding records, but the general feeling was "you can't rope a calf off a pedigree."

As the mechanical takeover of many of the horse's traditional jobs on the farm and ranch gathered momentum, however, many of the more dedicated breeders and ranchmen began talking about forming an organization for the perpetuation and improvement of this exceptional breed of animals.

In 1940, in Fort Worth, Texas, just such an organization, the American Quarter Horse Association, came into active being. The following year, the first registry and stud book was published.

Since that date, the growth of the breed has been nothing short of astounding. Today registrations of foals are at a rate of 60,000 a year, nearly four times greater than those of the Thoroughbred, the next largest breed in terms of registrations. This extraordinary boom in Quarter Horses, one which has spread to every corner of the nation, has been due, not only to the superior quality of the animal, but to the devoted men and women who have been, and still are, actively promoting the breed.

The Morgan Horse

If Justin Morgan sounds slightly unusual as a proper name for a horse, perhaps it is because the name originally belonged to a man—an impoverished, tubercular composer who eked out a living as a singing teacher and tavern keeper in eighteenth-century New England. And doubtless Mr. Morgan hadn't the slightest inkling of the fame that would one day come to the name when he journeyed to Springfield, Massachusetts, to collect a dark bay colt as payment for a debt. He called the horse Figure and in 1795 took him to Randolph Center, Vermont, where Mr. Morgan had decided to settle. Some researchers believe that on his arrival in Randolph Center the stallion was a two-year-old, but so little is known for certain about him that it is impossible to determine the precise date of his birth. Even Morgan "specialists" whose loving enthusiasm has led them to search out every conceivable source of information have not been able to agree on the year he was foaled. Some say 1789, others say 1790 and still more maintain he was born in 1793. Nor is there any less controversy about the identity of his sire and dam. Justin Morgan's son insisted that his father always labelled the colt a "Dutch horse," and numerous experts are convinced that he was indeed sired by a Dutch-bred stallion named Young Bulrock.

At odds with the "Dutch-bred" version is the testimony of another member of the family, John Morgan, who stated firmly that the sire was a horse of Arab or predominantly eastern blood and further specified that his name was True Briton. However, in centuries past, before formal registries and accurate stud books, horses' names often shifted about and it seems that the True Briton to which John Morgan referred bore a string of aliases including Beautiful Bay, Traveler and Hero. Even the name of Figure himself was completely ignored with the passage of time. As his fame spread, people at first began to speak of him as "Justin Morgan's horse" and then abbreviated this to "Justin Morgan."

Certainly of interest to adherents of the True Briton theory is the fact that at the time of Justin's birth there actually existed a famous blooded horse bearing this name. He was owned by James DeLancey, a New York Tory, and won acclaim for his racing speed by defeating a fleet rival known as Old England in a celebrated match race before the Revolution. During the war itself True Briton won even greater renown, much to the dismay of rebel colonists. His blinding speed and Mr. DeLancey's clever tactics resulted in daredevil exploits that confounded and damaged the Continental Army. To end the stinging setbacks, or so reports declare, one American patriot took matters into his own hands. With all the style of a Robin Hood, he simply kidnapped the horse and spirited him up to Connecticut where it is quite conceivable that True Briton might have sired Justin Morgan. At any rate, the unflinching tone of John Morgan's assertions, combined with other evidence, lends considerable weight to the proposition that Justin was sired by *a* True Briton, celebrated or obscure.

What little is known of the possible sire seems huge compared to what is known of the dam. She remains an utterly nameless mare probably native to the Connecticut Valley. A few clues suggest that she was a part-Arabian, part-Thoroughbred mare related to the imported stallion Wildair who was also owned by DeLancey. If so, her blood could explain the early quality of Morgans since recent descendants traced to Wildair through the maternal side include such important Thoroughbred sires as Nearco and Nasrullah. The Morgan Horse Register valiantly attempts to end the debate by accepting 1789 as Figure's official birthdate, True Briton as his sire and an undetermined Wildair mare as his dam.

Amid the forest of speculations, however, two points emerge as definite and unassailable. Justin Morgan actually did perform such incredible deeds as to rightly deserve his later role as a local folk hero and to engender an abiding affection for his breed in the region of Vermont. And, more important, he clearly was a sire of such prepotency as to leave his unique and indelible stamp on his descendants to this day, becoming the only single horse in history to found an entire breed named in his honor. His current legacy is some 15,000 members of the strain which are among the most amiable, durable and altogether functional horses the world has ever known.

The tragedy is that during his own lifetime no one could appreciate the full import of this phenomenal little horse. His value as a sire went unperceived until two generations of his offspring had matured and began to make a name for themselves. In the meantime a pitiful fate had befallen him. After Mr. Morgan's death, the horse was peddled around to a series of some dozen or so farmers, loggers and merchants who accorded him treatment that was anything but luxurious and in fact often abusive. Endless days he spent in harness, put to the drudgery of hauling, and after hours, to satisfy his owners' bills, he stood at stud for fees from $2 to $5. At the hands of his last owner, a farmer named Levi Bean, he was consigned to the ignominious task of dragging a manure spreader, and because he did not seem worth the barn space, was kept outside even in the dead of winter. Nevertheless, he remained healthy and fit and lived to the age of 32. Some accounts maintain that he was

Statue of Justin Morgan at the Morgan Horse farm in Weybridge, Vermont, owned and operated by the University of Vermont. (Vermont Development Dept.)

The Morgan's versatility is rivalled only by the Quarter Horse's. Here is a snappy fellow in harness at the Northampton, Mass., horse show.

killed by wolves, whereas others say he died from an untended wound caused by a kick from another horse.

Descriptions of Justin Morgan portray an animal of handsome quality whose conformation blended many Arabian characteristics with the traits of light-weight Dutch-bred drafters. His dimensions were those of a large-size pony, measuring to a height of 14 hands and tipping the scales at 800 or 900 pounds. His head was small and finely formed, his back extremely short and strong, and his tail set high and carried with spirit. These signs, as well as the absence of one vertebra observed on Morgan skeletons, would point to an Arab background but his heavily muscled legs, his massive chest and rounded barrel, and the hairy feathering around his fetlocks are indicative of a Dutch influence.

By whatever secret combination they were produced, these were the features that distinguished Justin Morgan and are the hallmark of every successor in the line. His children, regardless of how many generations removed they are from their forefather, are cast from precisely the same mold, even down to their coloring. Browns, bays and blacks abound whereas lighter colors, such as chestnuts, are less frequent and white markings are usually sparse and conservative. Indeed, even if Justin Morgan's exact pedigree were known and the many disputes over his true background resolved, it is unlikely that the facts would really account for his unparalleled influence as a sire. He simply surpassed the logic of blood-lines. He was a mutant, a genetic sport, a super-stallion the likes of which the world may never see again.

The multiple jobs admirably performed by Justin Morgan indicate that he was not only a Jack-of-all-trades, but a master of most. Everything he did, he did well—and with boundless generosity of spirit and kindliness of temper. He was the sort of horse that would let kids crawl all over him one minute and, the next, come off with the laurels in a whirlwind race. Of course in those days racing was a rather home-spun, informal and neighborly affair. The distance was usually 80 rods—a quarter of a mile. The horses started literally from scratch, a line drawn by a stick in a dirt road, and took off at the drop of a hat, which was the customary starting signal. Justin pounded through countless numbers of these events, running both under saddle and in harness, and all available information indicates that never once was he beaten.

Racing, however tiring it may be to a horse, was probably the closest thing Justin Morgan got to a holiday in which possibly he might have enjoyed himself. The rest of the time he was busy tearing rocks and stumps from the jagged landscape, plowing fields, raking hay, hauling logs to the mill, and carting assorted goods and harvests. After the burden of this was done, evenings would find him proving himself against all comers in weight-pulling contests. An eye-witness account states that in one of these matches the load was a tremendous log that horses of at least 1,200 pounds and more were unable to budge an inch. Justin

Morgan stepped right up, thrust himself against the traces and dragged the log off to the goal without stopping for an instant.

This very same versatility, plus a willing, gentle nature, has established today's Morgan as an exemplary pleasure horse, particularly appealing to an owner who wants one animal to fill a wide range of demands. His disposition makes him a perfect pet for children and although he still runs small in size, averaging a height of about 15 hands, his staunch durability enables him to take hard use by adults. The remarkable stamina of current Morgans, akin to that of their illustrious predecessor, is a particularly valuable asset on long trail rides in harsh terrain. Prior to 1951 when the United States ended its cavalry horse program, the federal government owned a Morgan horse breeding farm in Weybridge, Vermont, not far from Middlebury. Morgan stallions were raised to supply the remount service, as well as for use by private owners interested in stimulating the growth of the breed. To test the mettle of military stock, 300-mile endurance treks were designed, and in the course of these experiments government Morgans racked up astonishing records. Fortunately, the farm was taken over by the University of Vermont after the Government ended its program, and endurance rides have continued as an event wherein the might of the Morgan definitely prevails.

But by no means should it be inferred that the Morgan has been bred to muscle entirely at the expense of style. Present-day Morgans have an elegant show-ring refinement and, in action, can prance with a snappy, high-stepping air that duplicates the beauty of the Saddle Horse's gaits. In addition, Morgans may hunt and jump or, in western tack, happily take to the rigors of stock work. All the while the same horse will be at home in harness, too.

Given his unending array of virtues, it seems inconceivable that the Morgan could have come within a hair's breadth of extinction. Yet this is precisely what happened after roughly a hundred years of widespread popularity, and had it not been for the devotion of a few individuals who fostered the breed, the Morgan horse might have been forever lost.

A decisive blow was the coming of the Standardbred harness horse which was destined to join the Thoroughbred in a firm tyranny over racing. Prior to the Standardbred—from about 1800 until the end of the Civil War—it was Morgans who reigned supreme as speedy roadsters and harness racers and their kind was chiefly increased by Justin's three great sons—Sherman, Bulrush and Woodbury. Each of these lived to an age approaching dotage and this, combined with a natural prepotency, enabled each to sire hundreds of offspring forming three massive individual families. Bulrush was 36 when he died in 1858, and a son of Woodbury, named Gifford Morgan, is reported to have fathered some 1300 foals.

But of the three, Sherman was the most illustrious patriarch. It was Sherman's son Black Hawk who became the trotting champion of his

Sturdy yet smart enough for a lady's carriage, that is the Morgan. Here is a matched pair being judged at the Northampton, Mass., show.

time and, like his grandsire Justin Morgan, was never known to have been defeated. When he retired to stud, his $100 fee was a record figure and his earnings as a sire amounted to more than $34,000. Known in the Standardbred stud book as Vermont Black Hawk 5, it is indeed ironic that his blood was so instrumental to the rival strain that would eventually displace his kind in racing.

But Black Hawk's immediate successor to the trotting crown was his own son Ethan Allen, named Champion of the World after racing the mile in 2:25½. More glorious still in his splendid career was Ethan Allen's race against Dexter in 1867 at the Fashion Course on Long Island. Competing at the advanced age of 18 against an undefeated rival, Ethan Allen became a legend when he won three consecutive mile-long heats in 2:15, 2:16 and 2:19.

Such feats were scarcely isolated incidents. Similar Morgan performances had been astounding horsemen for many years and convinced any Doubting Thomases that the tales they'd heard about the original Justin were no exaggeration. It is, therefore, no surprise that for over a half a century Morgans alone dominated the harness field, both as racing stock and domestic animals perfect for milady's carriage. All the while they also retained their excellence as saddle mounts. When civil war came and horses were mustered for Union soldiers, Morgans were the only Northern cavalry mounts that could match the Thoroughbred and part-bred horses of the Confederacy.

The crisis came in the years that followed the war—a period in which the Standardbred, fortified by the blood of the Thoroughbred Messenger and Hambletonian 10, began to outstrip all other road horses. The problem was not simply that Standardbreds were faster than Morgans, but that in investing the strain with greater substance and endurance Standardbred breeders persistently turned to Morgan blood. Similarly, Morgan owners, hoping to reinforce the speed of their horses, crossed them back to Standardbreds. A fair exchange, or so it would seem, but in truth it all but liquidated the Morgan. For one thing, while the Standardbreds acquired the stamina of the Morgans, the Morgans never really came into the speed they hoped to acquire from the intermingling. Secondly, there was no Morgan register or any organized association to order standards for the breed, to keep vigil on Morgan activities and to officially record appropriate statistics. The result was that entire lines of Morgans simply disappeared into the Standardbred family, were swallowed up willy-nilly and listed in the Standardbred register with their own background completely dismissed.

Nor did the invention of the motor car do much to help the situation, for in threatening the position of all horses it nearly demolished the Morgan. That the breed managed to survive at all is largely due to the dedication of a handful of loyal patrons. First among them was D. C. Linsley of Burlington, Vermont, who tirelessly researched the background

Morgan mare and foal

of Justin Morgan and his offspring and published his findings in a book titled *Morgan Horses* brought out in 1857. He was succeeded by Colonel Joseph Battell of Middlebury. Battell's lifelong study of Morgans shed still further light on their history and culminated in the publication of the *Morgan Horse and Register* at about the turn of the century. In addition, he gave to the United States Government the farm in Weybridge to foster the breeding and betterment of Morgans.

Other indispensable supporters were Charles A. Stone and his son, Whitney Stone. Their reassurance and encouragement sustained the Morgan's fans through a dismal cycle of lean years such as 1925 when the meeting of the Morgan Horse Club, founded 16 years earlier, was attended by all of five members and annual registrations had shrunk to a scant 75. The efforts of both men became an inspiration to a whole new generation of horsemen and as the 1940's saw the nations of the world thundering into war, the homefront was witness to the quiet resurgence of the breed so long forgotten.

Once the rugged little Morgan was given a chance to catch on, nothing could hold him down. Registrations steadily mounted to reach a current figure of 1500 annual additions to approximately 10 times that number of Morgans already listed representing every state in the Union—with California now outstripping the Morgan's native Vermont as the leading producer of the breed. He can also be found in Canada, France, Spain, Israel—wherever there is still a need for a handsome, tireless little horse that puts his heart into everything he does. Indeed, if the Morgan has endured a perilous past, it has not been altogether in vain, for he has proved over two centuries of tribulation that the all-out willingness of his spirit and the vast number of his uses are truly inimitable qualities. They have earned him a place of such high regard in the community of horsemen that the future of Justin Morgan's progeny will never again be uncertain.

The Saddle Horse

Kentucky is famous the world over for two products: the Thorough-bred horse and bourbon whiskey. To followers of the horse, however, the bluegrass country is celebrated for a third product—another equine breed with equal claim to the hearts of old time Kentuckians as the Thoroughbred, which, having been "invented" elsewhere, is actually an adopted "favorite son." The true native of those parts is unquestionably the most stylish riding mount in existence, the preened and prancing Adonis of the show ring named the Kentucky Saddle Horse in honor of its birthplace.

The Kentucky Saddler, also known as the American Saddle Horse or simply the Saddler, Saddlebred, or gaited horse, is the essence of what in other circles would be termed pizzazz. He does not simply walk. He struts, raising his legs with dazzling animation, lifting knees and hocks to their highest reach, flexing at the pasterns so his hooves tuck sharply under, then striking earthward with all the authority of a dowager snapping shut her fan. His trot is a series of identical poses, first one pair of limbs soaring high, then the other in rhythmic succession to achieve a speed that is moderate but a look of hauteur that is unsurpassed. The canter is slow and graceful with legs still ascending in spirited elevation, never gaining speed or distance but placing on exhibit the artful flare and glamor of the horse. To quote an ancient maxim, the motion of the Saddler should be such that he "can canter all day in the shade of an apple tree." Indeed, this might well apply to the Saddler's every aspect, for the entire purpose of his being today is not to get anywhere in a hurry, or over anything larger than a twig. He is designed purely for elegance, a stylized showiness that leaves ringside audiences gasping in awe when they see him at official performances, and enhances the joy of the pleasure rider under less formal circumstances.

It is this explicit purpose that determines why the physical action of the Saddlebred is different from that of all other horse types. Since he is not expected to travel at speed and is not obligated to perform any job that would require him to cover distance with ease, there is no need for him to move with the low, horizontal extension of limbs which, as with the Thoroughbred, swiftly consumes the ground below. Instead,

65

he may concentrate his energies on the vertical, skyward reach that makes him a vision of fiery beauty chafing at restraint. And, to produce this effect, he is ridden with a definite restraining hand as can be observed from the attitude of his body. Literally gathered in by the reins, the Saddler's every step is a result of taut, controlled collection which, preventing the horse from going forward, forces the direction of his action upward. The chin is set and the impetus is from the haunches.

The unique talents of the Saddle Horse are shown in two distinct types, both members of the same breed and very nearly duplicates with but a single important exception. This essential difference is that one type adds to his repertoire two extra gaits which are called "artificial" gaits because they are cultivated by the human trainer and are not natural to all horses. This type of Saddlebred is referred to as a "five-gaited" horse and his brother is called the "three-gaited" variety.

The three-gaited Saddler performs only at the three natural, God-given gaits common to all horses. The slowest is, of course, the walk—a four beat cycle in which each hoof strikes the ground at a separate moment. The second gait is the trot—a two beat pattern in which the diagonal legs move in pairs. Right fore and left rear rise and fall in precise unison, followed by left fore and right rear moving simultaneously. The third gait is the canter which is a slow, collected gallop. Here the cycle consists of a three-beat pattern in which either of the front legs initiates the stride. If the right foreleg commences the cycle, the horse is said to be on the right "lead" and if the left leg proceeds first, he is on the left lead. For most horses these gaits are simply the gears or speeds whereby an animal gets from one place to another, but when performed by the three-gaited horse they become the controlled glory of a prima ballerina.

The five-gaited Saddler adds to these the "slow-gait" and the "rack"— both four-beat patterns in which each hoof falls singly to the ground in an easy succession so smoothly executed that the rider may sit comfortably in the saddle without bouncing or having to post. The slow-gait, in speed, is only slightly swifter than the walk and certainly nowhere near as brisk as the trot. In appearance, it is a true prancing gait wherein each limb in turn climbs high and precise, floats for a fraction of a second in mid-air, then falls to the ground before rising again. The horse performs under collection, every movement rigidly controlled. In fact the measure of constraint imposed on the horse is such that the careful listener can detect a slightly uneven rhythm to the footfall. Thus the landing of the hooves has a slightly syncopated timing and not an altogether metrical one-two-three-four stride.

The rack is virtually a high-flying version of the slow gait—and the only occasion when the Saddler really pulls out the throttle. At the ringmaster's order to "let 'em rack on" the five-gaited horse lets go with everything he's got and has been known to cover a mile in 2:19 when given more running room than the show ring can afford. His legwork

An American Saddle Horse working out at Dodge Stable, Lexington, Kentucky.

An American Saddle Horse being exhibited at the famed Devon Horse Show, Devon, Pennsylvania.

erupts into electrifying speed with none of his earlier rigid reserve. His feet seem to glide on invisible wings as he rushes faster and faster, still retaining elevation while moving into a free, fluid, precisely even one-two-three-four rhythm. It is a magical spectacle to behold, and though the Saddler makes his performance look easy, the gait is so highly culti-vated that it is one of the most demanding routines that a horse can be asked.

Still another branch of the Saddle Horse family is not shown under saddle at all but in harness. Known as the fine-harness horse, he performs in simple, unornamented show-harness drawing a lightweight four-wheeled vehicle. Though required to go only at a snappy walk and a moderately paced but lively part trot, his performance must always be obedient and courtly—especially at the hands of lady drivers. The nervousness some-times noticed in his relatives ridden astride must never appear in the nimble, mannerly harness horse designed for the elegance of the car-riage trade.

The conformation of the Kentucky Saddle Horse is as nobly fashioned as his gaits. His head is proud and well-formed, his neck long and swan-like tapering into an extremely prominent aristocratic arch that is also characteristic of the carriage of his tail. The most notable feature in the structure of his legs is the extreme length of the pasterns which permit the extraordinary springing flexibility of his feet. Through the barrel he is compact and rounded with full, solid muscling. The Saddlebred has always a plump, glossy, well-fed look with no trace of the lean angularity of the Thoroughbred, though both run to a generally tall size of about 16 hands. All members of the family are usually born to solid colors of black, bay, brown, chestnut and less frequently gray. Flashy white mark-ings commonly appear on the face and legs but not elsewhere. Three-gaited, five-gaited and fine-harness horses are almost identical structurally, except that the strenuous demands of the slow gait and the rack usually cause the five-gaited type to be somewhat fuller and more muscular through the chest and shoulders.

The destiny of today's top Saddlers to become show ring peacocks imposes on the horse the kind of hot-house handling, grooming and artful beautification that even a movie-starlet would probably find trying. The feet of the Saddler, a source of his vertically elevated action, are grown to extreme length and carefully weighted with heavier shoes to increase the animation of his legs. To create its uplifted arch, the tail is treated surgically. Except in certain states where this operation is now prohibited by law, the tail vertebrae are broken in such a manner as to produce a fixed and magnificently poised carriage once the tail is healed. To retain this effect the tail may afterwards be strapped into a brace that is worn whenever the horse is in his stall. Then, immediately prior to entering the ring, it is customary to have the horse properly "gingered." An attendant chews a stick of ginger until it gets to a pliable consistency and irritating taste, and then inserts it within the horse's rectum to prompt the animal further into keeping his tail aloft. For the five-gaited horse and his fine-harness relative, there is still an added touch. These two are shown in long manes bedecked with two ribbon streamers, and they are expected to have full, flowing tails. Should the tail happen to be of sparse growth, the horse is supplied a false one of sweeping, luxuriant proportions. For some unaccountable reason the three-gaited horse not only escapes the tail-piece but has the upper part of his tail shaved close along the bone and the lower part deliberately pulled into trimmer wisps. His mane is not allowed to grow at all but is roached directly at the neck.

If these measures tend to perturb the horse it is not to disadvantage, for if the rarefied beauty of the animal demands that he undergo certain discomforts, the fiery quality of his performance similarly requires that he be tuned to a sense of nervousness and excitement. Just as a race horse who is gentled risks losing his fierce compulsion to lead the pack, so the Saddler's sparkle may be dulled if he's turned into an indolent housepet. No two horsemen may agree as to whether the extreme means justify the end, but it cannot be denied that the ultimate result is indeed a creature of splendor.

Cruelty versus perfection is only one of the controversies that pursues the Saddler. A second debate questions whether he is fit for any other purpose than dandified strutting within the show ring, or whether faced with more rugged problems in life he could acquit himself honorably. It is wrong to assume that, because the highly trained Saddler is a fancy stepper, the breed consists of an assemblage of sissies. It has already been pointed out that the degree of cultivation involved in the gaits requires enormous endurance if the horse is to sustain his performance at length, making the Saddler an animal of proven stamina. Furthermore, in order for such a horse to be successfully taught his artificial gaits, he is obliged to possess an exceptional aptitude for training. His receptivity to learning is a basic characteristic not limited to a specific field, so that he can pick up the technique of jumping—or even working cattle—with the same ease as he learns the mannered airs of his orthodox routine. His educability, his stamina and the powerful muscling developed by his elevated action, often combine to produce a Saddle Horse with exceptional jumping potential. Much to the amazement of onlookers, he has even shown himself to be as good a mount as anyone can ask when ridden in the hunting field.

The utilitarian aspects of the Saddler are rarely put to any test today, but the fact remains that his origin was fully as dependent upon his usefulness as upon his attractive appearance. As the Daniel Boone era of Kentucky adventuring gave way to more peaceful forms of civilization, there arose a landed gentry of plantation owners—men who owned, managed and surveyed huge tracts of southern farm property. In order to administer their estates, gentlemen of this region required a durable,

A Saddler at the trot. Note the high action.

At the rack. Note the extreme collection.

obedient animal who could carry them on inspection journeys that lasted virtually from sunup till dusk. Given such long hours spent in the saddle, they needed an animal with relaxing, comfortable gaits that could be tolerated by both horse and rider without excess fatigue. Speed was not essential since landowners wanted to check their holdings without haste, but beauty was indeed a requisite as men of pride and local prestige were as intent on enhancing their public impression as today's patrons of Ford and General Motors The answer to this need was the development of a new breed—a horse whose great comfort, endurance and elegance would be eminently useful at work and openly admired at social appearances.

To arrive at this pleasant solution, Kentucky horsemen turned to existing colonial stock—Canadian and Narragansett pacers and easy-gaited amblers imported from England—and crossed these with the Thoroughbred, Morgan and Arabian strains. They relied heavily on the blood of imported Messenger and Mambrino and, during half a century of selective breeding, began to produce outstanding horseflesh that faithfully transmitted the desired qualities of the Saddlebred to successive generations.

Among the first great sires in the history of the breed is a Canadian pacer named Tom Hal who was foaled in 1806 and is said to have lived to the age of 41. Bought by a Dr. Boswell of Lexington, Kentucky, Tom Hal made a name for himself as a result of a wager by his owner. Dr. Boswell maintained that he could ride Tom Hal to Louisville, over 80 miles away by horse trail, between sunup and sunset. It was clearly no effort for Tom Hal to win the bet since after briskly completing his journey on the designated day he then repeated his feat the very day after, returning from Louisville to Lexington. At stud, Tom Hal not only founded a line of Saddlers that includes Bourbon Chief whose son, Bourbon King, is considered one of the greatest Saddle Horses of this century, but also contributed to the development of the Tennessee Walking Horse.

Though Tom Hal is a vital link to the background of the strain, the stallion officially specified as the foundation sire of the breed by the American Saddle Horse Breeders Association is, in fact, a Thoroughbred named Denmark. (The American Saddle Horse Breeders Association, so called since 1908, was an outgrowth of the National Saddle Horse Breeders Association, organized in 1891, whose early registries listed first 14 and then 17 founding sires. Later it was concluded that the most influential sire was Denmark and he was selected as the prime progenitor of the breed.) Though it is certainly true that Denmark was a remarkable stud in his own right, much of his claim to the title of foundation sire is due to his extraordinary son, Gaines Denmark. Gaines Denmark, foaled in 1851 out of a horse known as the "Stevenson mare," was an animal of such quality that he was chosen by John Hunt Morgan as his personal mount during the Civil War. It was prior to the war years, however, that Gaines Denmark showed his phenomenal capacity to produce fine Saddle Horse offspring. Statistics offered by the Saddle Horse register testify to what must have been a truly astonishing career at stud, for of the 7,311 listings in the first four volumes that trace their lineage to Denmark, 7,291 do so through families belonging to Gaines Denmark.

Challenging Gaines Denmark for honors as the top Saddlebred stallion of the period was a younger horse, foaled in 1863, called Cabell's Lexington. A descendant on his dam's side of Tom Hal and, through Black Hawk, of Justin Morgan, Cabell's Lexington proved not only to be a stallion destined to generate whole lines of famous show Saddlers, but also a topnotch performer himself. His success included triumphs over such rivals as Washington Denmark and Montrose—the former being a brilliant prodigy of the Denmark line who was undefeated until his bout with Cabell's Lexington, and the latter, also of Denmark blood, widely renowned for his beauty and the first of his breed to sell for the unprecedented fee of $5000. In all, Cabell's Lexington suffered but a single defeat in the ring—and that by a horse named Middleton's Drennon who was never registered.

Harrison Chief, sired by a Standardbred trotter and foaled in 1872, is another classic name in the annals of Saddle Horse history. Though he achieved his reputation in fine-harness and probably never had a saddle on his back, his breeding prepotency was such that he passed on to his heirs a quality that would be unsurpassed either under saddle or in harness. He boasted a horse show record that lists only four defeats and, more important, founded a clan of "Chiefs" that included champions in the ring and in the stud. It was his son Bourbon Chief who fathered the fabulous Bourbon King, a Saddler who became a twentieth-century legend. Bourbon King was a creature of such ultimate perfection that even the most optimistic observers reckoned his equal would not be seen within their lifetime, and their prognostications would have been quite accurate had it not been for a Saddler of more recent vintage known as Wing Commander. Owned by the superb horsewoman Mrs. Frederick Dodge Van Lennep and ridden by the nationally famous Saddle Horse showman Earl Teater, the incomparable chestnut stallion all but caused his audience to swoon like matinee idolators in his first electrifying performance on the big-time circuit at Lexington in 1946. His triumph in the three-year-old stakes was such that afterwards Carey Ward, a veteran Saddle Horse expert, said: "I never thought I'd live to see as great a horse as Bourbon King, but I've lived to see a horse that will be greater." In nine years of competition Wing Commander won over 200 championships. Among the incredible array of laurels was the winning of the World's Grand Champion Five-Gaited Saddle Horse title from 1948 to 1953 at the Kentucky State Fair, and from 1947 to 1954 at the Chicago International.

Now, of course, horsemen speculate as to whether they shall ever see the like of Wing Commander. No one can predict when or where the new monarch of the breed will be discovered, but one will assuredly appear. Meanwhile, the search itself will be a joy to the beholder. As any show goer with an eye for a ring full of beauties will agree, there is simply nothing to match the stylish display of the Saddler—a thrill that far outweighs any critical charges that might be levelled against this country's most significant native breed.

A Saddler at the canter. Note the vertical motion. The scene is the Junior League Show at Lexington, Kentucky.

The Tennessee Walking Horse

The Tennessee Walker, also called the plantation horse, is the downfall of every pleasure rider who ever resolved *not* to go overboard and buy a horse. There is a saying about the breed that goes "Ride one today and you'll own one tomorrow." The reason for the animal's appeal is the smooth, fluid, gliding gait for which he was officially named—an actual running walk which, in terms of comfort, not only has the edge on the Saddler, but possibly on one's own favorite rocking chair as well. Even the experienced horseman, newly transferred from the back of an ordinary walk, trot and canter horse to the back of a Tennessee Walker, is often struck with disbelief at the utter effortlessness of the ride. The ground, he can see, is swiftly passing by and he can clearly sense the brisk flurry of footwork going on below. But his own body, with or without the supportive grip of knees against the saddle, is almost perfectly still in an attitude of floating suspension.

The physical mechanics which produce this state of enchantment are closely associated with the rack and slow-gait performed by the five-gaited Saddle Horse. The footfall of each is an unmistakable four-beat cycle wherein the individual hooves rise and descend at separate intervals. The difference is that the Walker's gait is a true recognizable walk, accelerated and extenuated, while the Saddlebred gaits are so highly mannered that their relation to a normal walk is not so obvious. In the flamboyant parade of his specialized talents, the five-gaited horse may freely resort to every source of movement he possesses, and throughout the entire framework of his body each limb operates in coordination with its adjoining limbs. Back, shoulder, upper leg, lower leg, pastern and hoof all share equally the burden of propulsion so that while the rider may easily sit to either the rack or slow-gait, he nevertheless feels the natural shift and sway in the movement of shoulders, haunches and back.

The secret of the Walker's glide, however, is the isolation of his motion. By using the legs only from their juncture at the barrel downward, the upper shoulder and the surface of the back remain on a uniform lateral plane. The saddle is a virtually stationary perch which even an infant could stay on without strain, and the whole source of forward progression is four flying legs which feel wholly unrelated to a body that is miraculously still. The only other movement occurs at the horse's head which dips and nods, not unappealingly, as a result of the laboring to keep his body steady. The nodding head, common to all Walkers, is a characteristic by-product of the rapid walking gait and, if the horse should happen to relax his jaws, may occasionally cause an audible "pop" of the teeth as they are clacked together by the bobbing. At the normal walk, canter, or, less frequently, the trot—all performed with gingerly, animated action—the bobbing disappears altogether and the Walker approaches the regal, stylized glory of the Saddlebred.

The official speed of the running walk, as defined by breed specifications, is between six and eight miles an hour, but show Walkers travel at over twice this rate, not always to best advantage. For one thing, if the horse is pushed to excess he will lose the fine four-beat synchronization and slip into a rough two-beat pace or off-balance trot. Far more serious are the perils of what is referred to as forging. When a horse's legs extend horizontally into gigantic lengthy strides, all taken at four separate intervals, it is very common for a hind hoof, in the process of landing, to pass, by as much as two feet, the front hoof which is just about to rise. The harm comes if the feet collide. Unfortunately, at the breakneck show ring rate, the horse often has no time to worry about collision and Walkers have been known to emerge from a class with both front feet slashed to ribbons from ankle to hoof by the forging of his own hind feet. Now, happily, the overzealousness of their riders is being stringently corrected.

Even at more moderate speeds, the loose-limbed ease and serene beauty with which the Walker flows along is, at least in part, a noble deception. The illusion suggests that his running gait is a purely effortless gift when, on the contrary, the forced acceleration and limited use of the body require enormous strength to be sustained for the long distances which the Walker readily handles. The rigid demand for outright power is responsible for the thick, heavy muscling through the neck and chest of the plantation horse. In fact the hefty development of the forequarters, noticeably greater than that of the Saddlebred, is perhaps the only clue that might enable a novice to distinguish between the Walking Horse and the five-gaited horse when both are at repose. In other respects the two are so alike that even an expert eye finds it difficult to discern which is which at top-ranking shows where champion specimens of both types are assembled. Even the show ring Walker must tolerate the same beautification measures—weighted shoes, set and gingered tail with tail-piece and all the rest—as his five-gaited counterpart.

At a less exalted level, however, the Saddler emerges as the one who tends to retain the best of his breed's quality, while the plantation horse, at lower echelons, will incline toward coarser features and a rougher caliber of refinement. His head is somewhat plainer, his neck a bit shorter, stockier and nowhere near as prominently arched. His body is less com-

The Tennessee Walking Horse, like this fine specimen, was originally developed to carry overseers comfortably around the large Southern plantations.

pact and shapely, revealing a longer back and a barrel not as fully rounded. His tail is carried lower and his legs, which move with action that is less elevated than the Saddler's but has a more elongated horizontal reach, are inclined toward thicker bone.

Another rather curious hallmark of the Tennessee strain is the wise, wistful look of his eyes owing to the shape of eyelids which are often noticeably wrinkled and sloping. Eyelids so structured are neither exclusively or invariably found among Walking Horses, but so many of the breed share this expression that it has come to be thought of as one of their traits.

Unlike the Saddlebred, who appears only in solid colors, the Walking Horse has a widely varied coat that may be lavishly splashed with white markings on the body as well as the face and legs. Such widely ranging coloration, running from ordinary black, bay brown, chestnut and grays to more exotic roans, skewbalds, piebalds, and even palominos, is thought to be the result of the assorted crossings of bloodlines which figured in the background of the general plantation type until rather recent times when the Walker was finally distilled into a clearly defined breed.

While the more commonplace Walker's tendency to coarseness is detectable to the tutored judge, it is not severe, and enthusiasts of the strain should not be disturbed if an indifferently bred plantation horse is no more beautiful than an indifferently bred gaited horse. It has already been stressed that at higher levels the five-gaited Saddler and Tennessee Walker are barely distinguishable and, furthermore, slight coarseness is certainly no crime in any horse whose value rests on the performance he produces under saddle. In this respect it does well to remember that the Thoroughbred horse, that magnificent tyrant of racing speed, is largely thought of as being considerably less refined than his Arab forebears.

More important than hair-splitting details of conformation is that the Walker easily redeems any failings of the flesh by possessing a disposition beyond compare. It would not be so astonishing if his amiability were merely a trait of the well-handled family pet, but to find such gentle mannerliness in keyed-up show ring circles is all but unheard of. Yet even among finely blooded stallions, where bad behavior is common in every other breed, the gallantry of the Walker will result in impeccable conduct whether man, woman or child is at the reins. In fact, one Walking Horse owner admits to nearly swallowing his cigar upon discovering the secret activities of the frisky young stallion he regularly showed. It seems the horse was a favorite of all the local children, who talked the groom into letting them cool the stallion out, supposedly. Instead they sneaked him down the road a piece, climbed aboard his saddle-less back, and rode him to their heart's delight using nothing but a halter and lead shank for control. The Walker has been called the "gentleman of equines," whose kindliness makes skittish rivals look like mischievous delinquents.

That the Saddler and Walker fall prey to frequent comparison in which the former usually emerges as a paragon of beauty and the latter as a good Samaritan often makes their separate fans uneasy. The fans of the Saddlebred are afraid the public will think that all prize gaited horses are touchy, temperamental artifacts, and plantation horse fans fear people will think their champions are only close seconds in the realm of beauty. There are, of course, members of each breed which share the consummate good looks and virtuous character of the other. But comparisons are unavoidable, for the two breeds are linked not only by their extra-natural gaits but also by kinship in their history. The plantation horse developed in the same manner as the Saddler—through a prolonged period of selective breeding until the desired qualities were faithfully transmitted to its offspring. The Walker was Tennessee's answer to the needs of a "Gone With the Wind" tradition of agricultural gentry who desired a fashionable, durable, and comfortable mount to transport them to the farthest boundaries of their land. Once again, breeders of the region turned to the colonial stock available at the start of the eighteenth century and ran the gamut of crossings with strains more fully developed—the Arabian, Thoroughbred, Morgan, Standardbred and particularly the Saddle Horse. The same potent lines that shaped the course of the Saddler weave through the Walking Horse origins, with the Hals, Denmarks and Copperbottoms assuming a family prominence. With such a close affiliation of histories and almost duplicate uses, it is understandable why for many decades horsemen actually did not make any distinction between the Saddlebred and the Tennessee Walking Horse. In 1877, at the first Tennessee State Fair held in Nashville, there were classes for what were loosely described as "saddle horses." But by 1910 the Fair listed events for "plantation saddle horses"—the term "plantation" being used to designate the Tennessee type as opposed to the Kentucky type. Another nickname referred to Walking Horses as "turn row" horses, owing to the custom of examining the crops by rows.

Once the breakthrough was made in 1910 the plantation horse began to prosper as a breed in its own right, entirely divorced from its ties to the Saddler. A formal registry was established in 1935 when the Tennessee Walking Horse Breeders Association convened and, in researching the background of the strain, discovered that a vast proportion of Walkers originated from a Standardbred trotter named Black Allan. Officially specified as Allan F–I, Black Allan was selected as the foundation sire of the Walking Horse breed.

Black Allan was not only related by blood to Justin Morgan through a dam descended from Black Hawk, but shared many of the Cinderella aspects that marked the Morgan sire's life. Fate did not treat Black Allan kindly until his later years, long after a dismal early career in which he showed all the earmarks of a born loser. Foaled in 1886, he was a total loss as a trotter because he could not restrain himself from lapsing out of a trot and into a pace. Nor was there any improvement when he was raced as a pacer. It was years after all hope for him had been given up that the reason for his harness racing downfall was recognized as that which made him a towering progenitor of Walkers. Namely, he was simply unable to adhere to the strictly lateral strides of pacing in which both right legs and both left legs move in unison. Instead, his footwork fell into a syncopated cadence achieving a cycle of four separate beats rather than the two-beat rhythm of the pace. He was, in fact, racing with all-out speed in the demanding gait of the Walker. The result was two tattered and bleeding forelegs after every race, adding physical injury to the continuing insult of defeat. Scarred and supposedly useless, Black Allan was pawned off in a "good-riddance" trade in 1900 in return for $20 and a few head of livestock.

The next step for the luckless stallion would doubtless have been the cannery had it not been for James R. Brantly of Manchester, Tennessee, who checked Black Allan's breeding in the Trotting Registry and saw a glimmer of possibilities. He played his hunch and bought the stallion to breed to his excellent plantation mare, Gertrude. Their offspring listed champion after champion, including the most fabulous Walking Horse sensation of the day, Roan Allen F–38. (Though no one knows exactly when or why, the spelling of Allan changed to Allen.)

Roan Allen, foaled in 1906, lived until 1930 and became himself a creditable sire. But of all his accomplishments he was probably most celebrated for his phenomenal number of gaits. Witnesses swear that besides the flat walk, running walk and canter, he could perform the classic square trot, the fox trot (a somewhat unbalanced version of the square trot), pace and rack. About the only thing he couldn't do was an old-fashioned Dixieland Cake Walk. In all, Roan Allen was a seven-gaited wonder, a rarity that made him a star of his breed.

Another of Black Allan's dazzling sons was Hunter's Allen F–10, who proved his worth at stud by producing offspring that monopolized the stakes class victories at the Tennessee State Fair for over a decade. Between 1920 and 1933, 10 of the 14 first prizes went to children of Hunter's Allen, and the patriarch himself enjoyed a record in the ring that was not to be outdone by his juniors. He swept the highest honors at the Tennessee State Fair in 1912, when he was in his prime. But he boasted one of the longest "primes" of equine history, for in 1924, when he was 20 years old, he repeated his earlier triumph, defeating everything in sight including two of his own sons in a performance where, according to observers, he just plain "walked up a storm."

Tennessee is still the state where the cream of the Walking Horse population displays its greatest glamour, and the annual Walking Horse "Celebration" at Shelbyville is, in terms of the number of entries, the largest show in the country. But what is truly exceptional about the Walker is that he can bring his most valuable qualities to the less ambitious horseman without making an owner feel that in using his Walker for casual

Tennessee Walkers on a trail ride near Shelbyville, Tennessee. The Walker, unlike the American Saddle Horse, comes in a variety of colors.

enjoyment he is committing some sort of treason. The plantation horse is such a thoroughly delightful companion and so perfectly designed for informal pleasure, that even in the West and in dyed-in-the-wool Thoroughbred hunt country of the East he has won many devoted fans. Certainly it is not without reason that their enthusiasm may even exceed the devotion that surrounds him in his traditional home, so that now, in virtually every corner of the nation, the Walker is assured of the warmest welcome.

The Color Breeds

There is an old saying that "no good horse is of a bad color," but despite the fact that horse people have been assuring each other of this for generations, it has not eliminated superstitions about color that have existed for thousands of years. Arab breeders of ancient times were convinced that chestnut horses were the swiftest, bays the hardiest and paler-colored horses the least able to tolerate heat. In Elizabethan England the colors of the horse were related to the four cosmic elements of earth, air, fire and water, which were thought to influence the character of humans as well. Earth was the property of duns and blacks. Air was the controlling force of bays which made them "sanguine, nimble and pleasant." The chestnut, supposedly, was a creature of nervous nature and excitable spirit owing to the element of fire which dominated his temperament, while the pure white horse was influenced by water. Roan was the color thought to indicate the most harmonious balance of the elements. Numerous references in Shakespeare suggest that the Bard himself believed in the superiority of roans.

Even today there are horsemen who are persuaded that certain colors give clues to the particular virtues or shortcomings of a horse. It is not uncommon to come upon wranglers who'll vow that the best of all cow horses is the dun or the Paint. Bettors at the race track frequently wager

"I ride an old paint," says the song, and generations of wranglers swore by their brightly colored horses.

Paint stallion. The basic body color is dark with irregular white patches.

according to their theories concerning blacks and grays, insisting that grays are an omen of luck while blacks mean certain doom—or sometimes the reverse. There are some horsemen who fall immediately for the eye-catching features of a horse with a flashy coat, and others who are immediately suspicious of such an animal's true quality. The latter tend to wonder if perhaps, like a car with too much chrome, the fancy exterior may be designed to camouflage an interior that really isn't much good. Arising from such fears is the old wives' tale contending that white hooves, which frequently appear on legs that bear white markings, are not as strong as black hooves. The superstition is celebrated in an old ditty that goes:

> One white sock, buy him!
> Two white socks, try him!
> Three white socks, deny him!
> Four white socks and a white nose,
> Take off his hide and feed it to the crows!

The plain truth of the matter is that the quality and substance of a horse is neither affected nor revealed one bit by the color or markings on his coat. The single exception to this is the albino horse—the true white horse. Many people mistakenly assume that if a horse has a coat of white hairs, he is a so-called white horse. Actually, the majority of "white" horses are born black and turn grayer with the passage of time. Eventually such horses may lose the gray dappling or mixture of black hairs, leaving a coat that is white but is technically considered gray and should be listed as such on documents concerning the horse. The skin beneath such a coat, it can be observed, is the same grayish black that exists on horses of all other solid colors.

The albino, however, has a coat that is pure white from birth and beneath the hair is skin that is uniformly pink. Moreover, instead of the customary dark brown eyes possessed by most horses, albinos generally have pale blue eyes known as "watch" or "clock" eyes. Watch eyes often appear on horses with large splashes of white about the face; these horses have perfectly normal vision. Albino horses, unfortunately, suffer from the same weaknesses which plague all albino creatures, humans among them. They are notably sensitive to the sun and may have difficulties with eyes and vision. For this reason most horsemen are so skeptical of albinos that white horses have not found great favor as a color breed.

In all other instances the color of a horse and the pattern of his markings are not important—particularly if the color scheme consists of one of the standard, solid body colors and the usual white markings on the face and legs. The normal, accepted solid colors are:

BAY—May range from a yellowish tan called light bay, through a bright reddish color referred to as blood bay, to a mahogany shade called dark bay. Mane, tail and lower legs are black.

BROWN—Ranges from a lustrous, rich shade of brown to almost black. Brown horses which appear to be black over most of the body surface usually have light tan hairs around the muzzle and underbelly.

BLACK—A true, absolute pitch black which is rare.

CHESTNUT—Ranges widely from a light, yellowish red, sometimes known as sorrel, to a deep liver-colored hue with many red, gold and coppery tints in between. Chestnuts have a mane and tail that may be either a little darker or distinctly blonder than the body color, but they can be distinguished from reddish bays in that mane, tail and legs are never black.

DUN—A dull yellow-brown or tawny-gray. Duns have a black mane and tail and black legs—the last sometimes being marked by zebra-like striping. Duns commonly have a black dorsal stripe down the spine and, less commonly, may have a transverse stripe across the withers. The body color may also be imposed on any of the previously listed basic colors. When combined with black, brown or dark bay, the result is a smoky color called mouse dun. Imposed on light bay, the result is a sandy yellow called buckskin. Imposed on light chestnut, the outcome is the reddish yellow of the claybank dun.

GRAY—A mixture of white and black hairs which lightens with age and may range from a deep gun-metal hue to white. Dappling is common among grays.

ROAN—Any of the varieties of chestnut, bay, brown or black with a more-or-less even dispersal of white hairs running through the coat. Black roans are black horses with roaned coats, often hard to distinguish from grays. Blue roans are similar but have reddish hairs as well in the mixture. Red roans are bay horses with the mixture of white hairs, and strawberry roans are roaned chestnuts.

Head markings are:

STAR—Small patch of white on the forehead.

CALF FACE—Large, irregular splash of white covering generous portions of the face and frequently accompanied by one or two watch eyes. Calf-faced horses are also called bald.

BLAZE—A wide streak that runs from the forehead down the nose.

STRIP, STRIPE or RACE—A narrow streak that runs down the nose.

SNIP—A small patch of white on the lower nose or pink flesh color on the lip between the nostrils.

Leg markings are:

STOCKING—White reaching from hoof almost to the knee of the foreleg or the hock behind.

HALF-STOCKING—A stocking that reaches over the ankles but stops well short of knee or hock.

SOCK—A white anklet which reaches about to the fetlock.

Extensive research on horse coloration by Fred Gremmel of the Texas Experiment Station has brought him to the conclusion that but a single pigment is responsible for the entire variety of coat hues. This pigment is a light amber in color and may produce either darker or lighter coloration depending upon the amount present, the distribution of pigment clusters in the hair shaft and the density of the clusters. The clusters of a black coat are so thick that light is unable to penetrate, thus producing the black color. The position of pigment clusters in the hair shaft is also an

The Appaloosa is a definite breed which is able to transmit its coloring to its offspring. They are usually white over the hips and loin, with dark round or egg-shaped spots.

important factor. Among duns, for instance, all the clusters are situated on one side of the hair shaft causing the other side to have the watery, transluscent quality characteristic of the dun coat.

Much yet remains a mystery about horse coloration, but thus far it is known that the factors controlling coat pigmentation are hereditary color genes. In order for a horse to possess a coat of a given color, the genes required to produce this color must be present in the horse's ancestry. Let us take, for example, the race horse Whirlaway whose color was chestnut. One of his parents was a black horse, the other was brown. Of his four grandparents, three were brown—leading one to suspect that it would be most logical for Whirlaway himself to have had a brown or black coat. His fourth grandparent, however, was a chestnut, and it was these genes which prevailed to give Whirlaway his color two generations later.

This brings us to one of the curious facts concerning the color genes— namely, that certain color genes are dominent while others are entirely or at least to a large extent recessive. Horses of black, brown and bay, for example, possess dominent color genes which enable them to produce offspring of any other color traceable in their own background or that of their breeding mate. Chestnut genes, however, are recessive. If both sire and dam are chestnut, the foal will also be chestnut, regardless of the color of the grandparents—which explains why the Suffolk draft horse easily breeds to just this single color. Chestnuts breed so true that a non-chestnut Thoroughbred supposedly born of two chestnut parents will be refused registration by the Jockey Club.

The genes of the gray coat are about 90 per cent recessive. In other words, in matings where both sire and dam are gray, the color will pre-dominate among the offspring with exceptions occurring only 10 per cent of the time. Percherons, like the Suffolks, are another draft strain with a tendency to breed true to their color, producing a gray coat some 90 per cent of the time.

Albino genes are also recessive and breed true, causing the matings of an albino sire and dam to produce mostly albino young. In other respects, though, the albino is something of a puzzle. The majority of geneticists consider the albino a mutant—the term used to describe any creature whose characteristics result from some extraordinary and inexplicable change in genes from one generation to the next. Most mutants are re-garded as undesirable, but not all. Justin Morgan, thought by many students of the horse to have been a mutant or "genetic sport" in a variety of respects that did not include color, was obviously a case in which the strange change of genes produced only good. Polled Hereford cattle and numerous miniature dog types are other cases of advantageous mutations. In the case of the albino, the mutation is possibly caused by some mysteri-ous activity of the gene that dilutes coat pigment, thus effecting the com-plete absence of pigment. Whatever the explanation may be, it must take into account the fact that while the coat and skin of the albino contain no pigment, the genes required to produce color exist within the horse and are capable of transmitting color when mated to non-albino horses.

The complexity of the horse's color genes, even when confined to just the usual solid colors, is obviously far more intricate than that of such other domestic creatures as cattle and dogs whose color can, in most cases, be readily predicted and controlled by the breeder. The plot, as it were, thickens further by the addition of the three color breeds—so called because these horses are each possessed of extraordinary coat coloration not standard or common among the other breeds. These three are the Paint, the Appaloosa and the Palomino.

The Paint, also known as the Pinto or Calico horse, is characterized by a body coat marked with large, irregular patches of white set against any of the solid colors. If the color combination consists of black and white, the horse is also commonly referred to as a Piebald, and if white is combined with any color other than black, the horse may be described as a Skewbald.

Paints are further classified according to whether their coat pattern is dominated by the white splashes or by the colored splashes. The *Ovaro* type is a Paint whose solid color hairs appear as a base for the white patches. The *Tobiano* has a base coat of white and splashes consisting of the second color. Whatever pattern arises, the presence of these patches is a consequence of hereditary spotting genes. The Piebald effect, therefore, does not result in a foal merely because the lines of the parents contain genes capable of producing black hairs or white hairs. Actual "spotting" genes must reside within one parent horse's background and may, in fact, be present among horses of a solid color. Hence, if such genes are in the background of either sire or dam, it is possible for two horses of a solid color to produce a Paint. Since spotting genes are not yet certain to breed true, it is also conceivable for two Paints to beget a solid-colored horse whose spotting genes may not re-emerge for several generations. In the majority, however, Paint mares bred to Paint sires bear a healthy ratio of like offspring, making it attractive for color-breed fanciers to persist in the improvement of the quality of Paints and refine breeding stock down to a point where spotting may possibly be faithfully transmitted.

The association between "Old Paint" and the American cowboy or Indian is so familiar that there is a tendency to forget that Pintos have a previous history that extends far back into antiquity. Indeed, their color might be traced to prehistoric ages when the light and dark pattern of their coat was natural canouflage, like the zebra's, that blended into surroundings of patchy shade and bright sun. The existence of the Pinto is recorded by the Egyptians who depicted horses of such coloration on tombs as far back as 3400 B.C. In India, where they were known as the *Kathiawari*, and Tibet, where they were called *Tanghan*, it has been suggested that Paints were not just a color but, according to Carl E. Raswan, a distinctive type, rather like the horses used by the American Indians, with numerous Arabian characteristics. Mr. Raswan, author of *The Primeval Horse*, maintains that these Pintos were misbred to Mongolian and mixed-blood European horses, but later recaptured their quality when fresh eastern blood was imported by Moslem Indian princes and the British Indian Government.

There is ample evidence, too, that Paints existed in Europe at the time of the discovery of the New World. Father Bernal Diaz, the priest who accompanied Hernan Cortes and chronicled his explorations, specified that at least one Pinto was among the horses Cortes brought on his expedition to Mexico in 1519. Others obviously followed, eventually growing into a hardy, handsomely coated tribe of horses that soon found great favor with our native Indians, especially the buffalo hunters of the Great Plains. Whether or not the Comanches appreciated the decorative aspects of the Pinto, they doubtless profited from his camouflage, which is possibly why they got out the war paint and daubed additional splashes on a horse with inadequate markings.

In order to survive their wild life on the plains or, perhaps worse, the rigors of Indian use, horses had to be very durable, shrewd and shifty. The Paint, able to flourish under such conditions, rapidly earned the admiration of the cowboy, who occasionally paid a bonus of $50 for the purchase of this color breed in preference to an animal with a solid coat.

Whether by accident or by intent, when man first began breeding horses for qualities of speed and spirit rather than color, his selective matings tended to breed out Paint coloration. Thus, while flashy Pinto markings may appear on such recently resolved strains as the Tennessee Walker, coloration is absent in older breeds. There are no purebred registered Thoroughbreds, Morgans, Saddle Horses, Standardbreds or Arabs of Paint coat pattern—which, in snobbish circles, has caused the Pinto to be labelled some sort of mongrel creature. One can only caution such highbrows to beware. Thanks to the efforts of breeding organizations established only recently— such as the Pinto Horse Association in Ellington, Connecticut, founded in 1956, and the American Paint Stock Association in Fort Worth, Texas, founded in 1962—the quality of Pintos has improved by leaps and bounds, making them highly popular in a multitude of riding activities. When their sturdiness and handiness is crossed on Thoroughbred, Arab, Morgan, Quarter Horse, Walker or Saddle Horse blood, these "mongrels" have a conformation and performance good enough to lick the hide off more elaborately pedigreed competitors in the hunt field as well as the polo field, on the parade grounds and on the ranch, at the public show and at the private track where "brush racing" is the horseman's informal and popular test of speed.

The Appaloosa is another color breed whose body coat has dual coloration produced by hereditary spotting genes. Contrary to the Paint, who will have large and small, jaggedly outlined, irregular patches, the Appaloosa has a suggestion of uniformity to the pattern. The most obvious char-

Palomino parade horses at Mardi Gras in New Orleans.

acteristic is the nature of the spots themselves, for they are usually small, averaging about the size of a quarter or silver dollar, and tend to be round or oval on shape. The coat pattern may combine white with any other solid color, which, as it turns out, is frequently roan. As the Appaloosa Horse Club states: "Most individuals will be white over the loin and hips with dark round or egg-shaped spots. Spots vary in size from specks to three or four inches in diameter. Some Appaloosas carry the spotting all over the body, but it is usually dominant over the hips. Others will show white over the hips without the dark spots in the white. Still others will appear mottled all over the body, or will show white specks or spots with dark background."

Not only is Appaloosa coloration more uniform than Pinto patterns, but the Appaloosa, compared to his Paint relatives, has been more successfully resolved into a true breed, as opposed to a color, owing to his transmission of characteristics which appear even when the desired coloration fails to emerge. Thus, even in such instances when the polka-dot spattering does not result, all true Appaloosas are distinguished by three additional features. First, the eye is encircled by white, similar to the human eye. Second, the skin beneath the coat has a muddy, mottled pink and gray speckling that may be most readily detected around the nostrils. Third, the hooves are likewise parti-colored with vertical black and white striping.

In studying the history of the Appaloosa, it seems that the type's initial appearance was in oriental lands. There is evidence that such horses existed in Korea, Japan and India. In Persia they were revered as the sacred horses of the gods, and there are references in Persian literature to the warrior Rustam who rode a polka-dotted horse sired by a *dwi*, or devil. In China the strain was thought of as being the heavenly horse of Emperor Wu Ti, and horses of Appaloosa spotting have been discovered in Chinese art dating back to 500 B.C. Other relics unearthed in Italy also depict spotted horses and give reason to believe that the Appaloosa's forebears may have reached the European continent as early as 800. B.C. through an Etruscan migration. Whether or not they accompanied the Estruscans in the ninth century, it is almost certain that horses of Appaloosa coloration entered Europe via the Balkans with the army of Alexander the Great five centuries later.

By the beginning of the Renaissance, Appaloosas were fairly well spread throughout Europe and England. Spain, a major crossroads between occidental and oriental horseflesh ever since the Moorish invasion, boasted a concentration of Appaloosas among its Andalusan strain. Some animals with this identical coat were presented by Philip II to his uncle, Ferdinand of Austria, in 1560 and were included in the famed and elegant stud at Lipizza. Antique prints and etchings representing early Lipizzaners prancing through elaborate routines of the *haute école* show horses with unmistakable Appaloosa polka-dots.

With relative speed the spotted Spanish horses crossed the Atlantic and embarked into Mexico. Thence they traveled northward into the frontier terrain of the United States where they acquired their name and underwent successful breeding development at the hands of an enterprising Indian tribe. These superior breeders were the Nez Percé whose native terrain was in the region of the Palouse River (which, as applied to the horse, became Appaloosa) around northeastern Oregon and northern Idaho. Protected by the high mountain valleys in this area and profiting from better forage than was available on the plains, the Nez Percé enjoyed sufficient immunity from danger and ample grazing land to allow them to concentrate some effort on the rearing of horse stock instead of having to devote all their attentions to defense against hostile tribes. It has been reported that other tribes were indeed so envious of Nez Percé horses that, when not bent on bloody onslaught, they sometimes undertook to steal or barter for the Palouse type in preference to raiding Spanish stock. Commenting on the Nez Percé animals he encountered in 1806, Meriwether Lewis stated in his journal: "Their horses appear to be of an excellent race; they are lofty, elegantly formed, active and durable; in short, many of them look like fine English coarsers and would make a figure in any country."

About seventy years after Lewis's notation, a darker moment was to bring the Nez Percé horse to the attention of the white man. Led by Chief Joseph and superbly mounted on their Appaloosas, Nez Percé warriors made their last valiant stand against attack by the U.S. Army. Outnumbered five to one, the Indians were miraculously able to withstand the assault for five full days. On the sixth day, October 5, 1877, with their supplies depleted, the Nez Percé surrendered to a defeat which sealed the end of a noble tribe. Meanwhile their horses had so favorably impressed the whites that Appaloosa stock was swiftly snatched up. Of the total number, some 900 horses were lost during the long retreat while attempting to swim the flooded canyon of the Snake River. Approximately 1100 others survived, most of which were captured and sold to traders or grabbed off by settlers, while a few escaped to roam in wild herds.

With its members scattered and untended, the breed quickly fell into oblivion except for appearances in circuses and Wild West shows where their spotting was considered a fetching attraction. Everyone admired the Appaloosa but so few people were breeding them that by the 1930's the strain was a hair's breadth away from extinction. Fortunately, an article by Dr. Francis Haines, a foremost authority on the breed, appeared in the *Western Horseman* magazine and stimulated such interest and concern that the following year the Appaloosa Horse Club was formed with six charter members. The war years dampened activity but after the war the rise of the Appaloosa was incredible. In 1947 the club established permanent headquarters in Moscow, Idaho, and later formed its central stud book and registry. Within 12 years its membership has skyrocketed to include some 10,000 people, and horse registrations are currently being added at the astonishing rate of about 8,000 per year. At this rate of growth, Appa-

There is nothing the Appaloosa cannot do, either in Western or English rig. Here is a fine specimen doing some jumping in Abilene, Texas.

loosas have established themselves as being among the top five favorite breeds in the country, standing behind only such traditionally popular rivals as the Quarter Horse, the Thoroughbred, the Standardbred and the Shetland Pony. As a using horse, a pleasure horse or a show horse, there is nothing the Appaloosa can't do either in Western rig or English tack, and he has even made a mark for himself on the track where Appaloosas raced at the quarter-mile have been only a fraction off the Quarter Horse time. In short, wherever and however used, the Appaloosa has always given good account of himself and it is good to know that he is at last enjoying the admiration he deserves.

The third member of the color breed is the Palomino who, unlike the Paint and the Appaloosa, is not a parti-colored horse but has a coat of a single solid hue. At its most beautiful and desirable this coat should be precisely the color of newly minted gold and may be no more than three shades darker or lighter to qualify for registration. The skin of the Palomino should also be dark like that of other solid color horses, and both eyes should be the normal dark brown. White markings may appear on the face and legs but are forbidden on the body. Mane and tail are of a silvery white or flaxen color.

In further contrast to the spotted varieties, Palomino coloration can appear in any of the non-color horse breeds and does most frequently among Quarter Horses. More rarely, Palomino Arabs, Thoroughbreds, and Saddle Horses may once in a while crop up.

Research into the phenomenon of the Palomino's magnificent, glinting, golden coat indicates that the color is not transmitted by a specific, hereditary "Palomino gene," like the spotting factor that produces Paints and Appaloosas. Instead the coat results from a genetically incomplete dominance that is due to the interaction of three pairs of genes. These genes are: pure (homozygous) chestnut; mixed and impure (heterozygous) dilution; and either pure or mixed bay. Scientists explain that because the dilution genes, which are inherited from horses with a very pale or almost white coat, are mixed or heterozygous, it is impossible for Palomino horses to transmit their color faithfully and certainly when bred to other Palominos. Dr. M.E. Ensminger, a distinguished authority, says: "Genetic studies indicate that the color is probably unfixable, that it cannot be made true breeding, no matter how long or how persistent the effort."

In other words, when the three specific pairs of genes combine, they resolve themselves into a sort of stalemate that causes the dazzling Palomino color. Thus being hybrid in character, the qualities of the Palomino cannot be counted on to regenerate with 100 per cent fidelity among their own kind.

The necessary interaction that occurs by chance in the non-color breeds to result in an unexpected Palomino can, however, he induced with frequent success by at least four crossings. First there is the mating of two Palominos which produces an average ratio of two Palomino offspring to one chestnut and one albino offspring. Second, there is the mating of a Palomino and a chestnut which results in an average ratio of one chestnut to one Palomino. Third, there is the crossing of a Palomino to an albino which produces an average ratio of one Palomino to one albino. And finally, there is the crossing of a chestnut to an albino which produces only Palomino foals. Of the four methods, the Palomino/chestnut crossing produces the richest color and is the most widely preferred.

Historically the Palomino appeared often throughout many ancient lands. Howard Grekel, a student of the Palomino, declares that the writings of Homer and Virgil contain allusions to these golden-coated horses. Spain, as usual, acquired an abundance of them and it is thought that the Spanish themselves deliberately bred for the Palomino color. Spanish Palominos were known as "The Horse of the Queen" and their use was reserved exclusively for the Royal Family and forbidden to commoners. Palominos accompanied the conquistadors to the New World and rapidly became the favored mount of Mexican dons and prosperous hidalgos. At the end of the Mexican-American War in 1848, when the United States acquired California, many golden horses were discovered in the territory and Grekel suggests that the name Palomino is of recent origin—first appearing in written form around 1920—and was probably the ordinary Spanish surname of a local owner of such horses.

Two Palomino registries exist in the United States—the Palomino Horse Association, incorporated in 1936, and the Palomino Horse Breeders of America, organized in 1941. Their combined listings total over 25,000 horses. The prospect of ever refining the color into a true breed is now so dim, however, that many private pleasure owners do not bother registering their Palominos, thus causing a drop in the annual increase figures. This conceals the enormous extent of the Palomino's true popularity, for owners have discovered that the golden horse has proved his worth against every other light horse strain in endeavors that range from ranch work to pleasure usage to show competition. Since Palominos may be members of any of the recognized breeds, they are often gifted with the exquisite conformation of the various purebred types and may possess a clean refinement quite superior to that of other color horses. Their performance is equally outstanding with such winners as the world champion Quarter racer, Paleo Pete, and the world champion cutting horse, Cutter Bill, as evidence that the Palomino's fabulous golden exterior is not alone among his glories.

Paint stock horses near Groes Plains, Texas.

Standardbred pacers at Roosevelt Raceway, New York.

The Standardbred

To those who hail Thoroughbred horse racing as "the Sport of Kings," partisans of the harness racing game can answer that theirs is the pastime of a democracy. The exciting sulky sport that was born on the dirt roads of the new republic was brought to its present peak of excellence by rich people, poor people, and "just plain" people. More so than the Thoroughbred world, harness racing in this country still remains quite rural in character. While it does have its big city show-places like New York's Roosevelt and Yonkers Raceways, and similar racing plants in other large metropolitan centers around the nation, it is also perpetuated at more than 400 county fair meetings. And its "Kentucky Derby," the annual Hambletonian, is held each year in the small Illinois community of DuQuoin.

But harness racing is big business just the same. All in all it is an industry that represents well over a billion dollars in racing plants, breeding farms and livestock.

Unlike Thoroughbred racing, an import from England in our early colonial period, harness racing is a peculiarly American sport (one which, nevertheless, has been successfully exported to France, Germany, Russia, Italy, Holland, Scandanavia, Japan, Australia and New Zealand). The history of harness racing here goes far back into the American past. It began almost as soon as the settlers here had established a sufficiently adequate net of roads and turnpikes, thus making a better type of vehicular horse necessary. And the quality of these so-called "roadsters" improved apace with the highways.

The result was that the Standardbred horse of today, an animal which is just as "American" as is the sport, became the end product of a long and careful program of selective breeding, virtually all of which took place before the coming of the automobile

In Thoroughbred breeding, the aim is to produce maximum speed at an all-out running gait. In the case of the Standardbred harness horse, breeding is directed at producing the highest possible speed in one of two highly controlled actions—the trot and the pace. In fact, the name "Standardbred" is derived from the practice of qualifying to run only those horses which are able to equal or surpass a certain "standard" of speed. The wider meaning of the word "Standardbred" denotes a member of a family

99

designed to meet this standard. It is a family in which today breeding is as closely controlled and supervised as it is in the Thoroughbred clan. (A harness racer that is not a member of the Standardbred family can, it is true, be entered in a harness race if he can meet the standard. In such cases, he must be designated in the program as "non Standard." And he will be a rarity, indeed, so successful have Standardbred breeders over the years become in producing the very special horse adapted to this form of racing.)

Today, the "standard" is set at two minutes and 20 seconds for the mile. That's really travelling. But it doesn't approach the sub-two-minute miles which have been recorded by the fastest of the harness horses. The current mile record for the trot is Noble Victory's 1:55¾; that for the pace is Bret Hanover's 1:53⅗.

This naturally raises the question in the minds of newcomers to the sport as to just what is a trot and how does it differ from a pace?

The trot is simply a highly extended version of the conventional trot in that it is an even-beat, diagonally gaited motion. A pace is also an even-beat gait but it is just the opposite of a trot in that the pacer moves both left legs swinging foward in unison, then both right legs. This sort of action is described as a "lateral" gait. (In the language of the harness sport, this peculiar gait has caused pacers to be popularly referred to as "side-wheelers.")

A normal trot is a natural gait for any horse, but the 30-mile-an-hour clip of the racing trotter is not. This is because it is natural for a horse, when he is urged to greater output of speed, to break into a running gallop. "Breaking" in such manner is against the rules of harness racing, so the trotter must be bred and trained to resist this impulse and, instead, to greatly increase the tempo of his trotting gait.

The pace is not a natural gait at any speed, in the accepted sense of the word, although, through some odd quirks in their characters, horses have been known to pace on their own initiative. These, however, can be considered freaks. The Standardbred pacer is a horse that is bred with an inborn *tendency* to this motion. But it is a tendency that is exploited to the fullest only through the most careful schooling and "custom" making of shoes, toe-weights (clipped to the forepart of his hooves) and the elaborate harness in which he runs.

The Standardbred family of horses is today a "true breed" in the sense that when two are mated, they can be counted upon to reproduce their type in their offspring. Like many other breeds of light horse, the modern version of Standardbred has partaken deeply at the Thoroughbred fountainhead for much of his quality. But, despite outward appearance, he is a very "different" kind of animal. This is in part due to the fact that latter-day breeders have bred him selectively for different characteristics than are considered desirable in his Thoroughbred cousin—thicker, stouter legs, a longer back, and, generally speaking, greater pure ruggedness. It is also

The trot, a diagonal movement. The left front foot and the right rear foot strike the ground at the same time.

The pace, a lateral movement. The right front foot and the right rear foot strike the ground at the same time.

Standardbred mares and foals at breeding farm in upstate New York.

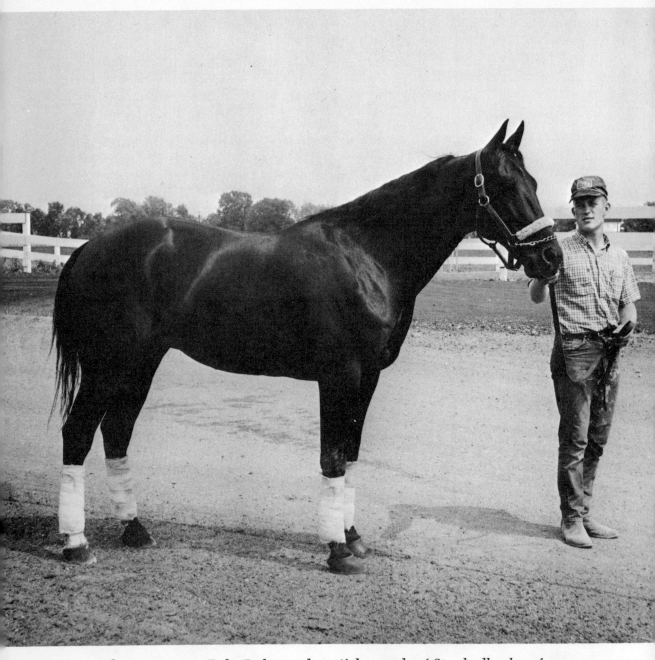

Champion trotter Duke Rodney, a beautiful example of Standardbred conformation. Although he has the fine look of a Thoroughbred, there is no doubt that this is a more rugged horse.

due in part to strains of other blood which account for his facility for trotting or pacing. Some of these were derived from antecedents, now wholly extinct, in England and in America.

In England, while the modern sport of harness racing has failed notably in attracting the public interest it has aroused in so many other countries, there was a time when the young bloods of that country enjoyed the sport of road racing, much as in this day and age, the younger generation enjoys the game of sports car racing. Special breeds of horses were developed, such as the Lincoln and Norfolk Trotters, to pull the light racing rigs used in this time. This period coincided more or less with the time of the colonization of the east coast of America and quite a few of this type of horse were among the first shipments of horses to Canada and to the original thirteen colonies.

From these, other similar strains like the Canadian and the Narragansett Pacers were evolved here and were well distributed even into the Virginia and the Carolinas before the colonists began to make use of the so-called "native" stock which the Indians had stolen from the Spanish.

Then this stock too was used in producing horses of unnatural gait. One such strain was developed in Virginia, and later in South Carolina, from a unique foundation sire of the Chickasaw Indian breed (a family of horses which was to play such an important role in the formation of the American Quarter Horse family). This was Col. Thomas M. Randolph's pacing stallion Hyatoga (sometimes "Hiatoga") and the horses developed from crossing his blood upon a strain of Canadian pacers known as "Copperbottoms" produced still another pacing family. Like the later Justin Morgan, these horses were named "Hyatogas" in honor of their foundation sire.

The importance of the Hyatogas is perhaps that they heightened enthusiasm for pacing horses rather than had a breeding influence of any real significance in the background of modern Standardbreds. All that can really be said of the Hyatogas and other similar families of this early day—the Bellfounders, Davy Crocketts, Tuckahoes and several more extinct "gaited" families—is that "they came and went."

But the passion for such animals remained. There were in the earliest colonial times, naturally, few roads smooth enough for any kind of harness racing. But among colonial dandies there was great enthusiasm for such horses as saddle mounts. (This is the heritage of our American Saddle Horses and Tennessee Walkers.) So numerous were these early American high-steppers, that visitors from abroad, who were more conventional horsemen, were moved to wonderment—and not infrequently to anguish.

Isaac Weld, a young visitor from Ireland, for example, was greatly distressed at what he found in Tidewater Virginia. "Some of the horses," he wrote, were "handsome, but for the most part . . . spoiled by the false gaits which they are taught." These "favorite gaits," he went on to explain, were a "pace and a *wrack*." The Americans, he said, insisted that the pace was a natural gait and that the foals paced as soon as they were born. Weld was dubious about that. "It is not one horse in five hundred that would pace without being taught." (The "wrack" he found to be "a gait equally devoid of grace, and equally contrary to nature.")

As the colonists of the late pre-Revolutionary era and later the citizens of the new republic reached a point in their road building that permitted faster and smoother vehicular traffic, the need for speedier harness horses grew. In the first half of the nineteenth century, a period in which harness racing itself took shape—this need was filled by the doughty descendants of Justin Morgan.

The earliest winners at state fair meetings during this time were such animals as Green Mountain Morgan, a grandson of the founding father, who won at numerous meetings in Kentucky, Ohio and Michigan. Even more distinguished was another grandson of Justin Morgan's, Black Hawk. Black Hawk is said to have been retired without a blemish on his record of wins. Although it is well thinned out, Black Hawk's blood (he is known to the Standardbred stud book as Vermont Black Hawk 5) still lingers in the families of many modern harness horses.

Thus, for almost all of the first half of the nineteenth century, these and other heirs of Justin Morgan dominated the harness racing field. But, in 1849, a sire came along that was virtually to rewrite the entire stud book of the harness family. This was a big, strong and, if we are to believe the accounts of most eye-witnesses, very hard-favored stallion who is officially listed as Hambletonian 10, but is much better known as Rysdyck's Hambletonian.

Rysdyck's Hambletonian first glimpsed light at the Orange County, N.Y., breeding farm of one Jonas Seeley. His sire, Abdallah, was a noted getter of good harness horses and his dam was a cripple named the "Kent Mare." Both sire and dam traced directly to the imported Thoroughbred sire Messenger. Messenger, when mated to blooded mares, was an important factor in the establishment of the American Thoroughbred dynasty. But Messenger was not always bred to ladies "of the blood." When he covered mares of the baser sort, as he frequently did, his produce showed marked ability between the shafts of a sulky. (This odd breeding ability to produce offspring of mannered gait was a quality, most students think, that Messenger inherited from his great, great grandsire, Blaze, who also sired Shales, the foundation sire of the Hackney Horse family of roadsters.)

At all events, Mr. Seeley was so displeased with his unattractive colt, Hambletonian, that he soon sold him to William Rysdyck, one of his hired hands, in exchange for Rysdyck's I.O.U. for $125.00. Had Mr. Seeley been able to foresee the future, he would not have parted with his ugly duckling for several thousand times that amount. Bill Rysdyck, after racing Hambletonian a brief time without any notable success around the fair meetings in upstate New York, retired him to stud.

Almost from the very outset, Hambletonian 10 was to establish himself as the greatest sire of harness racers that had been seen, either to that date

A pacer working out at Monticello Raceway, N.Y.

Harness racing at Roosevelt Raceway, N.Y.

or at any future time. In short order, his stud fee was put at the then astronomical sum of $500.00. He was at stud for 24 years and sired no fewer than 1300 foals. At this time, a speed of two and a half minutes for the mile was thought of as phenomenally fast—and indeed it was with the old-fashioned high-wheeled sulkies and slow tracks of that day. Nonetheless, some 40 of Hambletonian's offspring equalled or bettered this mark. So widely was he bred to the best harness mares during his long tenure of stud duty, that today something like 90 per cent of the Standardbred family can be traced to him.

From the time of Hambletonian 10 on, the breed and the sport improved rapidly. In fact, the modern-day standard of 2:20 for the mile was set way back in 1859 by an animal named Flora Temple. The introduction of "hopples" (the leg harness that keeps pacers from going off stride and "breaking") in 1885, and ten years later of the pneumatic-tired, low-wheeled sulky, brought about a feat that had theretofore been thought as impossible as we once thought the four-minute mile was for human beings. This was the breaking of the two-minute mile barrier. It was first accomplished in 1897, by the pacer Star Pointer.

During the era of repressive legislation a half century and more ago, when numerous abuses within the sport brought about the banning of Thoroughbred racing in all states except Maryland and Kentucky, harness racing was left almost completely alone by the reformers. Some years earlier it had acquired a similar bad reputation but had acted quickly to police itself from within before reform-minded legislators went to work on the sport. In fact, during these dark years in American Thoroughbred history, harness racing flourished as never before.

One reason that this form of racing caused no raised eyebrows among the straight-laced was that the animals were classed as "road horses" that did useful work besides just racing. (The owner of a Thoroughbred race horse could scarcely make *that* claim.) As a matter of fact, the "righteous" frequently could count among their own number many of the typical owner-drivers of the late nineteenth and early twentieth centuries. Many of the greatest names in harness history—horses like Lou Dillon, Star Pointer, and the great Dan Patch—were starring on the harness ovals when the Thoroughbred people were in the thick of their woes.

Of these, none stands out with the luminosity of Dan Patch, an animal who, in the minds of most keen followers of the sport, remains the greatest pacer, indeed one of the greatest horses of any kind, in history.

In the nine-year period in which he ruled the roost, Dan Patch did the mile in under two minutes flat exactly 30 times—an accomplishment which no harness horse has since duplicated. Making a mockery of the old two-minute magic number, Dan Patch once reeled off a sizzling 1:55 1/4, a record which stood for more than three decades. While the sulkies and tracks of Dan Patch's day were a great improvement over those of earlier times, they were still much slower than those in use now. Nevertheless, since Dan Patch set that mark, only Billy Direct in 1938, Adios Harry in 1955, Adois Butler in 1960, and Bret Hanover in 1965 ever went faster than that stupendous old brown champion, whose racing career began way back in the year 1900.

The coming of the automobile brought a sharp decline in harness racing. By the 1930's the sport had shrunk to the stature of being a minor county fair attraction, patronized, in the mind of the public at large, only by rustic die-hards. It certainly would have remained so—perhaps even have totally disappeared by now—had it not been for three important factors.

One of these was the introduction in the 1940's of the automobile-mounted starting gate which virtually eliminated the numerous (and boring) false starts which had marred the "action" of the sport over the years. This development, along with the general change-over from contesting each event in a number of heats to the modern Thoroughbred method of running single races, greatly speeded up the sport. And while there was the usual grumbling among the old-timers, the game became better suited to big city crowds, who were already devoted to the fast action of the running horses.

A second big reason for the resurgence of the Standardbred was the institution in 1940 of night harness racing. This began at Roosevelt Raceway, on Long Island, at the time a bankrupt auto racing track. Harness racing struggled along there during the war years, showed a meager profit in 1944, and the following year took off in a spiral of earnings to its shareholders that is probably unequalled in the history of sports promotion. (The total original investment of $200,000 is today estimated to be worth over $30 million.)

By operating at night, the harness racing people did not take on the formidable task of competing directly with the Thoroughbred tracks. (Thoroughbred racing at night, while it has been started at a few tracks, is generally viewed with disfavor by the running horse crowd.) The harness track operators, in this way, were able to bring out hosts of new horse fans—persons whose daytime occupations prevented them from attending the Thoroughbred tracks.

The third great influence in the rise of harness racing, particularly in metropolitan areas, is, of course, the seemingly inexhaustible supply of betting money that welled up in our post-war economy. This established harness racing really as complementary to, rather than competitive with, flat racing.

Harness racing, even in its most elegant form, retains its flavor as a "sport of the people," when contrasted with the Thoroughbred sport. But while the ownership of Standardbreds may not bring the social distinction that Thoroughbreds are thought to give to their masters, it does offer other attractions that more than offset those of pure snob appeal.

Not the least of these is money. While it is true that the cost of owning a harness stable is on the rise—yearlings are bringing as high as $60,000—

Trotters at Saratoga Raceway, Saratoga Springs, N.Y.

it remains a considerably less costly proposition than being in the running game at the owners' level. It is, in fact, an activity that one may enter for as little as a few thousand dollars. The horses themselves are much hardier, less subject to breaking down, and usually have much longer racing careers than do Thoroughbreds. Net losses to harness stables are fewer and net profits more common than in the Thoroughbred sport, where it is estimated that only some 3 per cent of stables show a profit in any given year. And harness purses have grown apace with the betting. Today, something like $50 million yearly is paid out in prize money, and big stakes events like the Hambletonian, the Messenger, and the Cane Futurity are now firmly established in the $100,000-plus category.

But there are other satisfactions in owning harness horses besides those of a purely economic nature. One is that of being able to participate actively—as many owners and their families do—in the training of a horse. During the morning workout hours, it is common to see the owner, his wife or even one of the children jogging the family trotter or pacer on his morning rounds.

It is probably just as well that they can pitch in and help with this part of the training, for by comparison with the Thoroughbred race horse, who is idle in his stall the great part of the time, the harness racer must be "worked" almost endlessly to stay in racing trim.

As with any other breed of horse, the Standardbred's success at the track will depend upon the sum of his physical gifts and the will, or "heart," with which he puts them to work. Apart from these considerations, it can be said of the Standardbred perhaps more than of any other horse that an extreme sense of discipline and a maximum degree of fitness are also absolutely necessary for victory.

He is halter "broke" almost as soon as he is foaled. In the latter months of his yearling days, after he has been bridled and has grown used to having a bit in his mouth, he is gradually "tacked up" in the complicated harness he will wear at the track. "Line driving" is the next step in his schooling. In this procedure he is controlled at a walk by extra long reins handled by the trainer who steps along behind him, turning him to left and right, starting and stopping him.

When he has grown accustomed to this sort of direction, he will be put between the shafts of a jogging cart, a heavier version of the racing sulky, and gradually stepped up to a pace of about a mile in three minutes. During this period, great attention is paid, as it will be throughout his racing career, to his shoeing. There is a wide assortment of shoe weights and types for harness horses. One of these will be best suited for each individual animal. Then there are also the "toe weights" attached to the hoofs of the forelegs which will help him extend his stride. These too are selected, after experimentation, for the exact weight needed by the horse in question. In this phase of his schooling, the harness racer will work as much as four miles a day three times or so a week.

Standardbred mare and colt having a romp. Generally, Standardbreds are much more economical to keep than Thoroughbreds.

If he is coming along well, his trainer will now reduce the workouts to perhaps twice a week but put greater stress on stepping up his speed until he reaches or surpasses the 2:20 qualification mark making him eligible to race.

The strenuous workouts, however, do not cease or even let up much after his racing career begins. Even on the day of a race, he will usually be worked once in the morning. And the night of the race he is almost always worked three more times, twice in front of the jogging cart and, finally, hitched to the racing sulky. This final "work" of a mile will be but a few seconds slower than the actual tempo of the race.

To those accustomed to "flat" racing, the harness sport is often quite puzzling. For example, the newcomer often wonders why in the earlier phases of the race all the horses are often brought into Indian file along the rail, seemingly without making any effort to pass one another. What is happening is that each driver knows just how much he can "use" his horse in the course of the race and is conserving the animal's energy, while saving ground, for the moment when he must make the move that can decide the outcome.

Then too, the reins seem to be very tightly held even in the final dash for the finish line. The reason for this is that the driver, going at a 30-mile-an-hour clip, must take extreme caution in steering his horse so that he will not swerve at close quarters and cause a dangerous pileup on the track. Also, exactly the right amount of restraint must be used to keep the horse from "breaking" out of the trot or pace into a gallop. When this happens, the driver must take his animal to the outside and may not attempt to improve his position until the correct gait is restored.

One thing about harness racing is certain—that is, that far more than in the Thoroughbred sport, it is the working partnership of man and horse that makes for victory. Many are the Thoroughbred trainers who, watching through their binoculars and seeing a jockey blunder away a possible win, wish they had been able to "make the weight" and ride the race themselves. In harness racing, where the almost frictionless character of the racing sulky makes weight a factor of little importance, the trainer is very frequently also the driver. Unlike the jockey who may have never seen his mount until it is time to go to the post, the harness driver usually knows his horse intimately. Driving a harness racer is unquestionably a far more precise science than is riding a flat horse. And it can be safely said that in this game, the better driver, even though his animal may have less potential, can and often does win over a superior animal whose reinsman has less ability and experience. Probably for this reason, there is no other form of horse racing that brings as much satisfaction to its participants.

Horses Great . . .

Anyone whose past includes some memory of the muscular titans of the heavy horse strain laboring tirelessly at their work will recall these stalwart creatures with a special twinge of affection. To some the sturdy drafter brings back memories of a time when cities had not yet turned to asphalt but were laced with random cobblestone lanes—a time when the soft glow of old gas lamps lined narrow curbs after a dusky sky had darkened over low roof tops and chimney-pot spires. At just about this hour came the ragged clip-clop of the brewery hitch or the merchant's team jogging homeward after the day's delivery rounds. To others the draft horse brings recollections of lush fields swelling ripe with the harvest. Here the towering plough horse was seen, his body spattered with dark gobs of mud, his head set low and determined, his hulking shoulders shoved deep into the collar, his ears flickering back to share in the traditional private discourse between farmer and horse.

Except in completely undeveloped regions, such scenes have vanished from America. With one swift thrust the invention of the combustion engine made the faithful dray horse the first sad victim of automation. To his admirers the loss of the heavy horse as a practical, working animal has been all the more painful in that his decline was so abrupt and relentless. As recently as 1937 the working draft stock employed in England numbered over a million horses. Approximately two decades later the figure plummeted to about 70,000 and has since decreased even more. A similar nose-dive has occurred in America where the heavy horse was once so vital a commodity that one out of every two horses registered belonged to the draft horse family. Now the annual additions to purebred registries total less than a thousand among all breeds combined.

Despair at his passing is deepened also by the realization that of all the horse types encountered in history, none has had a more glorious past or an influence more crucial to human events than the horse which is now a forgotten hero. From the fall of the Roman Empire to well after the discovery of the New World, the mighty Great Horse was an instrument in the destiny of all Europe. Like the sword, the shield and the coat of arms, he was a symbol of personal worth and honor—and, more important, the indispensable means to armed conquest. Even though his valiant role in

A pair of Belgians haying near Zearing, Iowa.

the romance of medieval times has long since been eclipsed by his humbler use in agriculture, his powerful, rough-hewn countenance still suggests an elemental dignity that links his heritage to the legends of Camelot.

However unfamiliar the observer may be, he cannot mistake the heavy horse for any other possible type. The draft horse is characterized, above all else, by sheer, massive size and brawn. He is, among horses, a veritable giant who easily runs to an average height of 17 hands and often an almost incredible 20. His weight is equally impressive, frequently mounting to an even ton, which is roughly twice the poundage of a Thoroughbred race horse. His head is rugged and handsome and makes no pretensions to a delicacy that would be inappropriate to his size. Coarse by contrast to lighter breeds and sometimes Roman-nosed, his face would be an awkward sight on any other horse, but on the draft horse it has a look of splendor and integrity. His legs are thick, indestructible pillars leading into hooves as large as dinner plates. These limbs may be quite long, but they sometimes give an impression of squatness due to the dimensions of the frame they support. Beginning at the neck and extending to the rump, the body of the heavy horse is a beefy, bulging muscular extravaganza. So plump are his haunches, so mammoth his shoulders, so cresty his neck, and so full and solid his chest and mid-section that nowhere except at the withers and larger joints can ordinary protrusions of bone be detected. Yet despite the immensity of his conformation and the crushing power of his brute strength, his is possibly the most placid, willing and kindly disposition of all domesticated creatures. The least temperamental of other breeds can, occasionally, go sour and stale through boredom, careless handling or overuse. But hour after hour, field after field, burden after burden, the heavy horse faces his chores with an amiable reliability and an almost professional concern for getting a job done well.

The heavy horse gained his first prominent triumph in 378 A.D. when, at the Battle of Adrianople, Goths armed to the teeth and mounted astride ponderous cold-blooded horses overran the legions of Rome and sealed the defeat of the Empire. The concept of massive armored onslaught that brought about the Gothic victory was somewhat new and alien to the practices of mounted armies in the Mediterranean area. Heretofore cavalry forces of the Trojans, the Greeks and Romans rode into battle only modestly sheathed in protective apparel—a shield in hand, cuirass and helmet, and perhaps greaves on the lower leg. Mounted agility and soldierly athletics were heroic feats among these warriors. A tactic known as the Parthian shot was a typical example of the early horseman's skills. In this maneuver the horseman deliberately rode past the enemy he'd selected as his target, lulling his victim into thinking he'd missed the chance to get off an arrow and that the moment of danger was past. Then, with truly astonishing mastery, the horseman whirled on the back of his mount and, while riding backwards at full speed, released the unexpected arrow. Naturally the animals used for such techniques had to be swift, light and nimble, and these were readily available in the lands bordering the Mediterranean Sea.

As the fall of Rome merged into the Dark Ages, the philosophy of warfare changed. The tribes of northern Europe, long held more or less in check, were now unleashed to wield their own power on their own terms. Their might consisted chiefly of wild hordes mounted on heavy native horses and protected by heavy armor that at first consisted of hides and wood. When the dust finally settled, however, the mounted armies of Europe were made up of an exclusive order—men of noble birth who wore, like the troops of William the Conqueror in 1066, a mesh of body armor made up of interlocking metal links and solid iron helmets.

The burden carried by the horse grew to be enormous. Plate armor supplanted mail, and the total weight of rider and armaments often amounted to some four hundred pounds which completely eliminated light-framed horses from service. What was needed, instead, was an animal of tremendous power and size to take on the rising load. Stock for the provision of such an animal was readily available in the form of descendants of Equus robustus—an ancient species that roamed the forests of Northern Europe in prehistoric ages. Thick-boned, cold-blooded, coarse and lumbering, he produced offspring of like characteristics but whose parts gradually blended into a less crudely conformed whole. This type always remained native to Europe and, except when horsemen intentionally experimented, was almost entirely free of the influence of oriental blood. The earliest defined strain to emerge from this background was the Flemish horse, founder of all subsequent draft breeds and distinctly related to the modern Belgian.

Once his virtues were recognized by the French, the Flemish horse came to be coveted by his Gallic neighbors. Stock that could be captured or bought in Flanders was taken back to France and produced a type which came to be known as the Norman horse. Norman horses that remained in France gradually established an exceedingly handsome heavy horse breed familiar to us now as the modern Percheron. Other Norman horses, recruits in the cavalry of William the Conqueror, were taken to England and mated with island animals—mostly the English Black Horse. Their descendants formed the basis for the three modern draft breeds of the British Isles— the Shire, the Suffolk and the Clydesdale. These three strains, plus the Belgian and the Percheron, constitute the major breeds among present-day heavy horse types.

Today the association between the draft horse and agriculture is so firmly established that it may seem rather curious that the heavy horse existed over a thousand years before really being introduced to farming. One problem, of course, was that his military value in the Middle Ages caused him to be a high-priced luxury far beyond the reach of any peasant farmer. One scholar has pointed out: "The destriers, or trained battle-chargers, able to carry the immense weight of the heaviest armed nobles, cost around £100, or as much in modern purchasing power as a high-

A Percheron stunt horse performing in the Barnum and Bailey Circus, Madison Square Garden, N.Y.

A pair of draft horses takes a holiday from farm chores to participate in a pulling contest at the Iowa State Fair, Des Moines, Iowa.

powered limousine." Nor was their keep any less extravagant. In 1310 one archbishop complained of the expenses involved in supporting England's Great Horse population, stating that the weekly sum spent on each steed would feed four or five people.

Further delaying the use of the drafter as a plough horse and worker in the fields was the peasant farmer's traditional use of oxen for these purposes. For centuries the ox had been yoked and hitched to all manner of cart and plough, and though the working pace was slow and plodding, medieval farm plots were so small, isolated and primitive that speed and efficiency were not necessary. Then, too, the ox had advantages which the horse could not compete with. When the best years of his service were over, the ox could be slaughtered for food and skins—a fate which horses had more or less escaped since prehistoric times. Thus, the valorous Great Horse took second place to the lowly ox as an agricultural tool.

Among the few peaceful functions which the heavy horse *did* perform was his role in travel which, in medieval days, was primarily by horseback. Riding palfreys were often noted for their comfortable "ambling pace" and one sensitive lady was horrified at having to accept "a cruel trotting horse" instead of her usual ambler which carried her and her infant child on a pillow. Carriages were drawn by sturdy heavy horses—Percherons who pulled the French diligences and, in Germany, a light-weight descendant of the Flemish horse which subsequently developed into the German Coach Horse.

The draft horse type was also used to turn mill wheels—a thankless job of endless circles made all the more horrible by the custom of blinding these animals in order to prevent dizziness. Other unfortunate creatures were tormented by inhumane versions of our present-day hauling contests. Hitched to green trees, rival contenders were forced to pull until the loser collapsed flat to the ground in exhaustion or death.

A pleasanter life fell to the heavy horses used to deliver the mails, often ridden in the sixteenth century by a mounted courier who signalled his comings and goings by sounding a horn. Subsequently coaches transported the mails and these too relied on animals of draft horse background.

It was between 1700 and 1800 that the agricultural revolution arose in full force. Lord Ernle, commenting on the impact of these years, says: "England not only produced food for a population that had doubled itself, as well as grain for treble the number of horses, but during the first part of the period became, as M. de Laverque has said, the granary of Europe." Nor did activity dim toward the end of the eighteenth century. Inspired by the Crown, large landowners lent their enthusiasm to agricultural development and George III himself delighted in being referred to as "Farmer George." Mechanical inventiveness provided better ploughs. The flail was replaced by the threshing machine and mowing machines were designed. Once the implements of labor were produced, the heavy horse found his natural niche as the power that would wield them, and by the nineteenth century organized breeding and agricultural societies were being formed to share their knowledge and selectively refine valuable horse stock. The five magnificent strains they perfected were imported to America where, as the burgeoning young country pushed westward, these stalwart creatures tilled the vast wheat belt, tamed the fertile wilds that would feed the nation, and became a tool of our survival.

An interesting characteristic of modern heavy horses is that while their origins share much in common, the five strains developed distinct individual differences not only of conformation but of color as well. Colors and markings are not absolutely fixed but there is a trend for each strain to breed to something of a pattern and to a structural type that distinguishes one from the other in a manner that is somewhat unusual among horses linked so clearly by both blood and usage.

The heaviest of the five is the Belgian, who is not, however, the tallest. His weight is a staggering 1900 to 2200 pounds and in height he runs to 17 hands or a little under. He is, as breeders say, the most "drafty" looking of his kind—that is, excessively wide through the chest, deep through the barrel, and muscular through the quarters. He is unmistakably broader and blockier than other drafters and has a compact, short-coupled back and a body that seems to have thrust itself down deep into big, chunky legs. Belgians are, in fact, so husky through the barrel that when they move they often roll or "paddle" from side to side and have no trace of springy, elevated action observed in some of the other breeds. Built for absolute maximum power, the beauty of the Belgians lies in their incredible strength rather than their exterior. In color, sorrels, chestnuts and roans are most common and these frequently have white blazing on the face and flaxen mane and tail. Blacks, bays and grays occasionally appear but are viewed with disfavor in most breeding competitions.

As mentioned earlier, this breed is directly descended from the ancient Flemish horse and is regarded as being of pure European extraction with no oriental infusion in the bloodlines. Imported to America at a rather late date (in 1886 by Dr. A. G. Van Hoorebeke of Illinois), Belgians were slow in gaining favor and were at first criticized for having stubby hooves, round bones, short necks and other flaws of over-all coarseness. These have been corrected by selective breeding, causing the Belgian to become enormously popular among heavy horse experts and resulting in annual registrations that now average about 400—almost twice those of any other heavy horse strain.

The Shire is the tallest of the drafters, measuring to a height that is often a good two or three inches bigger than the Belgian while their weight is about equal. Quite opposite to the Belgian, the Shire is long and rangy with an extended frame that has little suggestion of the round, chunky conformation that stamps the earlier breed. His immense height makes the Shire tower above all other horses and he is further characterized by the heavy growth of hair that sprouts in tufts around his fetlocks. These

Belgians at a Milwaukee circus parade.

hairy thatches are called "feathering" and are also found on the Clydesdale who, along with the Shire, is sometimes referred to as one of the "feather-legged" breeds. Shire coloration runs most commonly to bay, brown and black, but grays, chestnuts and roans also appear and are not penalized for their color in the show ring. It is usual for Shires to have white markings on the face and white legs from knee or hock to hoof.

The Shire gets his name from the shires of east-central England where, especially in Lincoln and Cambridge, the strain was originally developed. Indeed, the Shire doubtless owes much of his handsomeness and exceptionally well-formed structure to the fact that he was among the earliest of the Great Horse types to be developed especially for agriculture. Robert Bakewell (1726–1795), revered as one of the first major influences on English husbandry, took a keen interest in the breed and gave the Shire an early footing through his efforts to develop and refine farm livestock. Shires were imported to Canada in 1836 and a stallion named Columbus was brought to Massachuetts prior to 1844. It was during the 1890's, however, that Shires enjoyed a sweeping popularity which has, unfortunately, long since declined and left the breed with only slender increases in current registrations.

It is hard to imagine a creature weighing between 1,600 to 1,800 pounds as being something one would call "cute." Yet the Suffolk, smallest of the draft horse breds, has, in his unpretentious, almost homely look and his irresistably winning nature, an appeal that has made him a traditional favorite on the farm and caused him to be thought of as a member of the family. The Suffolk is readily recognizable by his modest height which runs to an unspectacular average of 15:2 to 16:2 hands, and it is common for the breed to measure higher at the croup than at the withers. An additonal trait is a uniformity of color, for the purebred Suffolk always bears a coat that is some shade of chestnut. White markings, if they appear at all, are very small.

Historically the Suffolk is unique. He is the single horse among the heavy horse tribes whose pedigree extends back to one prepotent sire known as the Crisp horse. This stallion, foaled in 1768, was owned by a Mr. Crisp of Ufford, England, and it has never been determined whether the breed first got its color from this progenitor or from earlier interminglings with light-colored Norse horses. Another feature of the breed's development is that the Suffolk has always been associated with strictly rural use, giving valuable assistance to the farmer and keeping his distance from merchants and urban commerce.

If the Suffolk lacks the glamor and majesty that makes other drafters more impressive, he possesses qualities of his own that have firmly established him as the treasured friend of the working man. His comparatively small body possesses a mighty strength. His attitude is steady and persevering, his heart generous and affectionate, and his appetite easy on the feed bills. For such reasons as these the Suffolk was widely exported from the region in England where he was developed and named, and the strain was in such demand in British Commonwealth countries that shipments to America were rather limited. Thus the roughly 3,000 registrations in the United States do not indicate the Suffolk's true popularity here. His numbers are found in many parts of the globe where he is remembered with enduring fondness.

What the Saddle horse is among light-horse breeds, the Clydesdale is to the heavy horse family—a snappy, strutting model of elegance prized above all for his high style and fashionable looks. Since he was raised in the valley of the River Clyde in Lanark County, Scotland, it is not surprising that the Clyde is heir to exceptional beauty, for the Scots are well-known for cultivating handsome livestock, such as their Aberdeen Angus cattle and Black-faced Highland sheep.

In motion the Clydesdale is characterized by the definite springy action of his legs, an arched and graceful elevation that is like the gaited horse's airs. In fact, over-all, the Clyde's way of going is more flashy and animated than that of other drafters, and his is the only breed in which competition animals shown in hand do not require an assistant to follow behind urging the entry into more spirited performance.

Clydesdales do not ordinarily run to great weight. Averaging from 1,700 to 1,900 pounds, they are only slightly heavier than the Suffolk. Standing at roughly 17 hands, the breed has a generally rangy conformation that would be quite similar to the Shire's if Clydes ran to the same immense height. Shire-type feathering grows luxuriously around the fetlocks but among Clydesdales is particularly long and silky and fluffy. Dominant colors are rich browns and bays with white markings on the face and legs.

Initially Clydesdales were imported to America from Canada but drew so much attention that by the 1870's they were being shipped over directly from Scotland. From the outset they enjoyed a wide following and particularly caught the fancy of prosperous urban merchants who proudly reflected their success in the great matched hitches and teams used to transport their goods. The glamor of the Clyde has always been able to turn an ordinary beer delivery into a public event enjoyed by gathering spectators. Now used in exhibitions and parades, Clydes still inspire awe.

Also known for his extraordinary beauty is the historic Percheron, a creature of subtle lines and harmonious structure who, in recent years, has been overshadowed by the flash and fancy manners of the Clydesdale. First imported to the United States in the 1850's, Percherons found an overwhelming reception and for decades were the most widely distributed of all the draft breeds. So valuable a purchase were they that businessmen bought them as investments, and there once was a time when there were more registered Percherons in the United States than horses of any other breed. Total registrations were an almost incredible quarter of a million horses, giving clear evidence of the Percherons past value even though current interest has slackened off.

The height of the Percheron runs from 16 hands up and his weight ranges from 1,900 to 2,100 pounds, making him neither as large as the Belgian and Shire nor as light as the Clyde and Suffolk. In color fully 90 per cent of the breed runs to black or gray.

Among the heavy horse strains, the Percheron stands unique for the class and quality of his conformation. He is, to be sure, tremendous and muscular, but he lacks any of the ungainliness associated with the other breeds. His build strikes one as being all of a piece—neither stubby nor blocky nor long and rangy. In motion he neither waddles nor lumbers nor struts, but goes with clean, balanced, spirited, natural strides. He looks, in fact, rather like a well-constructed riding horse simply magnified in size, and he has the refined characteristics—perfectly proportioned to his stature—that one would seek in the lighter breeds.

Largely responsible for these physical endowments is the extensive infusion of Arab blood traceable in the Percheron's background. His native home is the northwestern section of France called La Perche and, like the other breeds, he is originally descended from the Flemish horse. But unlike the other strains, he has been crossed extensively with oriental horses and has acquired the fine, intelligent-looking head, delicately molded ears and trim legs of the eastern type. His superior looks have served the Percheron well, for he has been fully as active in coaching as he has been in farming and was favored as an elegant carriage horse in the days of the Bourbon kings. Today he not only is a star performer in the circus but is considered a valuable resource in the breeding of hunters and jumpers. Commonly used to beget size, substance and power in the offspring, he also transmits a placid and amiable disposition ideal for use with hounds.

The interests of the majority of horsemen are now far removed from these five great strains and the fact that they are being sustained and perpetuated is due to the noble energies of a handful of breeders, agricultural schools and private patrons. Deep thanks is due them all and applause for a keen enthusiasm that more than makes up for their small numbers. Were it not for these devoted supporters we would no longer be able to enjoy the excitement of old-fashioned horse-pulling contests which still flourish at fairs, expositions and shows in rural regions from one end of the country to the other. Whether the entries are pedigreed prize-winners or humble, homebred drays, and whether they are pulling a trusty old stone-boat or the modern hydraulic tension release rigs mounted on trucks for such events, these contests are always sensational crowd pleasers. Lively cheering (and sometimes lively wagering) greets the towering drafters as they compete by turns to see which can pull the greatest weight. And their majesty prevails as ever in the fabulous matched hitches of the Anhauser-Busch brewery Clydesdales and imposing Shires of England's Whitbread brewery hitch—horses which bring to today's parades and ceremonies the breathtaking color and pageantry that surrounds their ancient heritage and which, for over a thousand years, enriched the story of civilization.

And Horses Small

In following the history of the horse, it is interesting to note that the very existence of certain breeds was seriously threatened by the coming of the internal combustion engine in the early nineteen hundreds. Yet 50 years later, in an era of space satellites and lunar probes, the horse has emerged as a dynamic force in the huge recreational "industry." The Thoroughbred, through racing alone, represents so·sizeable a leisure time investment that this single strain has become an economic lifeline for numerous states. And in the realm of the "just plain horse" of undetermined origin and no particular talent other than an ability to provide enjoyment, not even the Federal Department of Agriculture can reckon exactly how many are owned and how much money is spent in their care. But the figures are large enough to establish that ownership of a horse is well within the means of any family which can spend in the area of $1000 a year for outdoor recreation. Indeed, this represents an average cost for board at a commercial stable and is easily cut by nearly half in rural communities where the proprietor cares for the animal right at home.

The generous figure of $600 which feeds and supplies a full-sized horse is sliced again a third by the pony. By definition a pony is any horse whose height does not exceed 14.2 hands, and it is largely owing to his size and light touch on the feed bills that he is a popular and suitable pet for any family with a patch of backyard, a shed for shelter, obliging zoning laws, and roughly $400 to keep him in hay and a very sparse outlay of oats. In other words, given a half-acre of paddock and a 10′ by 10′ shelter, the annual upkeep of a pony amounts to the equivalent of a modest dinner for two each week. Thus it is not surprising that in some areas of the nation, ponies are as frequent a household addition as the dog or cat.

Though the pony is small in size and requires but meager maintenance, it is altogether mistaken to think of him as the second-rate model who lives in the shadow of the large and exalted horse. Financially, a top pony of the highest breeding potential can out-price a large percentage of Thoroughbreds seen on the tracks. The dazzling little Shetland stud, Frisco Pete, was purchased for no less than $90,000. As to stylishness, the nimble, glossy little Hackney Pony is a snappy stepper, fully as spectacular as anything in the world of harness horses, and, in the field of athletic competi-

127

Shetland mares and a foal at Fernwood Farm in Illinois.

tion, still other pony types reveal themselves agile jumpers.

But the quality about ponies that commands the greatest respect—and which, in fact, is what makes them such a great pleasure to own—is their rugged individualism. The pony, by nature, is able to bear all things. However fat and sassy the pampered show ring miniature may seem, he was very likely born of a race that evolved and handily survived on some pitiless rockbound island in the dank cold of the North Atlantic, or perhaps on a ragged stretch of mountain along the coast of Wales or Ireland. Somewhere he has a relative whose forage consisted of seaweed shreds, washed-up kelp and soggy march grasses in bordering sea swamps—dismal rations that could not support large-sized horse-life. With an indomitable will to live, the wild pony conquered his natural surroundings by adjusting to them. Through the centuries his size diminished, his woolly coat thickened, his determination set, and his hardiness became invincible. To this day, regardless of how highly cultivated the descendants of the wild strains may be, these heirs possess an extraordinary turn of character, a deep drive from the past that motivates an instinct for self-preservation. (As a parent recently suggested, perhaps it is this instinct rather than the pony's appealing size that accommodates him to children.) Thus it is something of a disservice to dismiss a dapper little pony type with the mere acknowledgment that he's "cute." With deeper awareness of what the wild strains have withstood and surmounted, we discover an incredibly stalwart, self-sufficient, enduring quality that makes some part of even the tiniest Shetland the mortal equal to Gibraltar.

The Shetland Pony is by far the most popular of all pony breeds, with some 40,000 purebreds now listed in the American Shetland Pony Club registry. It is impossible to estimate the many more unregistered and cross-bred Shetlands which also abound. Engaging, mischievous, eager and playful, his innate brightness and charm, plus a size that officially must not exceed 46 inches and is sometimes as small as 26 inches, make the Shetland a star attraction among children. In addition to being the favorite of the pony strains, his history is most typical of the past that shaped the general course of all ponies.

The Shetland pony, or "Sheltie" as he is often called in the British Isles, was originally a wild ancient strain native to the Shetland Islands off the coast of Scotland. The earliest indication of his presence there was furnished by an archaeological find unearthed in Scotland in 1864. This relic is a slab of chloride slate engraved on both sides in bas-relief with Celtic characters and representations of small horses and riders. Known as the Bressay Stone, the object dates from the Celtic Christian period before the Norse invasion (about 800 A.D.) and establishes that the Shetland tribe preceded the Vikings. A further clarification of the pony's pre-Norse existence is furnished by references of the conquerors themselves. One of the areas where Shetland ponies abounded was commonly called *Hrossey*—Horse Island—in chronicles of the Norse, and, although there are frequent allusions to the animals discovered there, not a hint has been found to suggest that the Norsemen imported them. Thus it can be safely concluded that Shetlands existed as far back as 600 A.D. and, in a larger form, perhaps even prior to that.

The mystery that arises is how they got to the Shetland Islands to begin with. Perhaps they were the seed of runaway Roman horses who ventured far to the north. Or perhaps their ancient forebears were cold-blooded northern European horses shipped ashore in some unrecorded voyage of an even earlier date. In all probability, whatever the nature of the primitive stock on these islands, they were later visited by horses of prominent eastern blood—perhaps transported by errant Spanish ships. There can be no doubt that both hot- and cold-blooded characteristics are to be found in the Shetland—to the extent, in fact, that virtually two distinct types have emerged within the modern breed. The Island type, favored in Britain, retains the colder, coarser look associated with the heavy horses of Northern Europe. In America, the more delicately featured oriental appearance is preferred and cultivated. Thus one can assume that either the original stock was a mixture of both oriental and northern blood which eventually developed into two different types, or that an initial body of cold-blooded animals was later influenced by oriental newcomers.

It is certain that once these animals arrived at their new habitat they were evermore to face a life of hardship. There is a saying about Shetlands that "they are born on the heath, they live on the heath, and they die on the heath." Subsisting all this while on rough heather and washed-up vegetation from the sea, it is small wonder that their official top limit in height is under four feet. And, given the icy climate they live in, it is not surprising that they have developed a unique coat to protect them from the cold. The long, shaggy hair they grow in winter is only the top layer of a thick protective covering, for underlying this is a heavy wadding of almost sheep-like wool—especially noticeable in younger ponies. Not until the pony foal is about two years old does this wool begin to thin out and be replaced by hairy fur more like the normal equine coat. Left in the wild as they are, it follows, too, that there is an endless range to the Shetland's coloration, with mouse gray, dun, cream, black, bay, brown, chestnut, gray, white, spotted and dappled animals appearing regularly.

The Island type, still used as a pit pony in English mines, has a conformation resembling the draft horse. His head is proud but rough-hewn, his limbs short and stocky, his forequarters solid and chesty. The American branch of the family, in accentuating all the classic eastern qualities, has legs which though short are dainty and slender. His body is compact and well-proportioned. His neck is often arched and his head so highly refined that his face often dishes inward like the Arabian's. Petite little ears are barely visible among great thatches of mane that will still grow rampant when left unpulled, but given the luxury of blankets and stabling his coat becomes sleek and fine with barely a trace of his poor relation's shaggy fur.

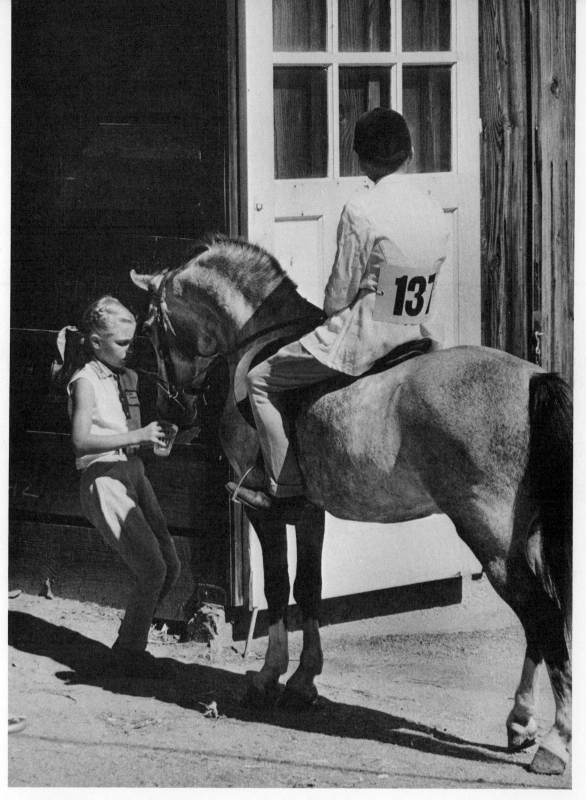

A Welsh pony preparing for a class at the Devon Horse Show, Devon, Pennsylvania.

Shetland yearlings at Fernwood Farm, Illinois.

In the United States, where the Shetland is a treasured member of the family, his versatile talents are exploited to every conceivable effect. For pleasure he is ridden in both Western and English tack. With hooves trimmed down and tail held naturally he becomes a perfect children's pony hunter and is shown in such classes over two-and-a-half-foot jumps. But when his hooves are grown long and weighted, and his tail is set into an arch, he is transformed into a dazzling fine-harness pony—another of his show ring specialties. More recently he has even come into his own as a racer. Attached to a light sulky and going at the trot, he is now the featured performer in the rising new sport of pony racing. Assuredly it is in harness that the Shetland can most readily be enjoyed by his adult fans, but not because he is unable to bear the weight of mature persons. Many a husky Shetland owner has first demonstrated his own strength by picking up the pony, then demonstrated the pony's by stepping aboard for a breezy ride. But in addition to looking like an A.S.P.C.A. official's nightmare when carrying a large rider, the Shetland's short-legged strides produce a gait that is simply too brisk and choppy for the comfort of an adult. Under saddle he is the domain of children, but the fact that he easily takes to the carriage or cart makes him fun for all.

Though the Shetland ranks highest in popularity, there is an increasing interest in numerous other imported pony breeds, among the most important of which are the Welsh and the Connemara. Strictly speaking, Welsh ponies are even more distinctly divided into two categories than the Shetland. One is the Welsh Cob, a large-sized and recent pony descendant of the old Welsh cart horse. It is not known whether the Cob was ever expressly influenced by trotting horse blood, or whether he simply took to the trot on his own, but it is apparent that his talent at the gait is considerable. His trot is effortless and speedy and for this reason the Cob is primarily a driving animal, particularly valued as a roadster.

It is the Cob's older hill-country relative, more accurately known as the Welsh Mountain pony, who has captured the fancy of American horsemen, and any reference in the United States to the Welsh pony applies to this strain. Like the Shetland, the Welsh pony is an ancient, wild, native type that originated in barren, craggy country and was used for labor in coal pits. But whereas the Arabian influence on the Shetland has never been specifically identified, it is known for fact that approximately a century ago a selection of Arab stallions were set out to mate freely with Welsh pony mares as the first of several measures taken to improve the quality of the breed. The eastern infusion has left an unmistakable stamp—a sensitive, chisled, dished face; prominent, intelligent-looking lowset eyes; small tapered ears; and a highly arched, crested neck that wedges deep into strong, sloping shoulders. Through the body the Welsh pony is short and well-coupled, his tail is set high and carried with an air of pride. His gaits are characterized by a spritely animation, a naturally spirited action that is again reminiscent of the Arab.

In height the Welsh pony runs, on an average, noticeably taller than the Shetland and the official upper limit of 12:2 is a full hand greater than the Sheltie's permissable top size. Also on the whole, the Welsh pony has a physical appearance that is more conservative than the Shetland's. His coat, even in the wild, does not grow to such woolly, shaggy lengths and his coloration is usually solid, with grays, whites and chestnuts appearing frequently in the United States. Spotting among purebreds is so rare that when observed it tends to arouse suspicions as to the quality of the pony's bloodlines.

The taller size of the Welsh strain, the solid thrust of his naturally animated legs, and the inherent muscular power of his fore and rear quarters make him a splendid pony hunter in the field as well as in the show ring. He possesses a general quality of handiness—to say nothing of extreme good looks—that is of great value to younger hunting members. He is a naturally safe, agile jumper and can easily cover three- or three-and-a-half-foot fences. The snappy elevation of his footwork and the fine Arabian cast of his features also make him perfect material for use in fine harness. For use in harness, of course, his feet are grown and weighted and his tail is set.

Among the tallest members of the pony family is a strain found on the west coast of Ireland among the sharp peaks and ragged crevices of the Connemara Mountains in County Galway. Aside from having a lilting name, the Connemara has a patient, amiable nature that in itself might have been inspired by some gentle, wistful poet. He is a friend to all, with malice toward none, so that even though his taller size—between 13 and 14.2 hands—causes him to tower over a tiny Shetland, he is often a far more placid, even-tempered mount for inexperienced children. Indeed, his height is a definite asset for any parent given to eyeing his child's pony with a glimmer of envy. The 14-hand Connemara, fortified by the traditional hardiness of all ponies, is a charming mount for ladies or moderate-sized gentlemen, attractively proportioned to carry the larger rider and with enough length to his strides to create smooth, pleasant gaits.

Particularly striking in the Connemara's conformation is his resemblance to the Thoroughbred hunter—or, specifically, that ideal hunting type which is a cross of Thoroughbred on colder blood. He is not altogether lean and angular with the fragile, deer-like limbs of the racing Thoroughbred, but in proportion to his size he has a distinctly rangy, horizontal frame that is different from the round, short, collected look common to both the Welsh and Shetland strains. His motion also recalls the Thoroughbred, for his strides are of a low, pendulous, extended, ground-covering nature. Indeed, given his limited stature, the Connemara is capable of goodly speed—sufficient to make Cannon Ball, the first foundation sire of the Connemara stud book, a well-known trotter of his day. Clearly, however, the Connemara was never designed to make his mark in harness. His speed has since been far surpassed by highly bred trotters and, lacking the dapper animation of the Welsh strain, he brings no particular lustre to the role of fine-harness pony. Yet if ever there was a creature born for hunting it is the Connemara. He has all the size and free-wheeling reach to keep his young rider right at the forefront of a brisk, demanding pace, and he has precisely the bottom and substance to handle rigorous hunting terrain and fences as solid as steel. In fact, when it comes to jumping, a good Connemara has more natural brilliance, dexterity and common sense than practically any other horse or pony. One of the great open jumping champions of all times and a show ring darling of the 1930's, was a 56-inch flying wonder named Little Squire. Carrying a full-grown man and easily sailing over fences upward of five feet, this handsome little Connemara put to shame competitors a full two hands taller, and to this day Little Squire remains a legend among the professionals who specialize in jumping.

Though coaching was once just an ordinary means of transportation for persons of even modest means, it is now in the equine world what *haut-couture* is to fashion. Luxury for the privileged horseman is ownership of such handsome, lightweight, lofty steppers as the Cleveland Bay or Hackney horse. The drawback is that one must not only be able to afford the horse, the team or entire hitch, but the harness and the vehicle and have access to grounds suitable for a rather elaborate type of outing. Thus it is readily understandable why Hackney and Cleveland Bay coach horses are a rare sight in America. Fortunately, the ultra-elegant pony version of the Hackney horse reduces the complications somewhat, and, in any case, is so irresistible that he has kept alive spirited heavy-harness competition at horse shows. He has, in fact, become a brilliant, glorious synthesis of all the color and pagentry once associated with coaching.

The heavy-harness animal differs from the fine-harness animal in that the latter is used strictly as private pleasure stock rarely required to perform tasks of more than a trivial nature, or to make trips that are more than just slight domestic sojourns. Fine-harness stock, horse or pony, wears harness that is delicate, draws a lightweight vehicle, and is bred for manners and brilliance.

The heavy-harness coaching type, however, had an actual professional calling in that he once provided public transportation. While on the one hand, the Hackney horse was expected to present a stylish, prosperous-looking appearance, he was also expected to draw solid, cumbersome diligences through all manner of English roads, including mud that was sometimes hub deep. Emphasis was not only on attractive conformation, but on power and speed. The power and sheer brute strength was supplied by the heavy horse blood which exists in the background of the full-sized Hackney, and the swift, traveling gait of the coaching type resulted from crossing with the old English Norfolk trotter. Later, Hackneys of this basic Norfolk trotter and heavy horse background were crossed with classic stallions "of the blood" (that is, valuable eastern imports) that assumed so prominent a place in English breeding of the seventeenth and eighteenth centuries.

Blaze, foundation sire of the Hackney horse, was foaled in 1733 and is a grandson of the Darley Arabian. Condensed, as it were, from a breed whose pedigree is illustrious, it is obvious that the Hackney pony is not in any sense a wild strain but is of a distinguished and cultivated ancestry.

Most of today's Hackneys are bred with a show ring destiny in mind and have become the dandies of all the pony clans. Glossy, glamorous and regal, the Hackney moves with breathtaking elevation and exaggerated, springy flexion of the pasterns. His neck is muscular and highly arched, his head held high and proud with eyes that have a bold, nervous, intelligent look. His tail is docked to a decorative brush and his hooves are worn long and weighted. Curiously, however, though he may be as primped as a fashion model, he produces a sense of infinite power, a mammoth muscular strength that is a holdover from his heavy horse background and more or less alien to the fine-harness types. Possibly it is this unusual combination of power and delicacy that makes the Hackney such an exceptional beauty. Straining against the bearing reins and a polished but real working collar, drawing the classic phaeton or perhaps a gig, he is clearly no fragile cream puff. His legs thrust and snap with authority, rather than hesitantly rising and floating—a sure, determined step that summons up all of his ancient heritage.

Averaging a height of 12 to 13 hands, Hackney ponies invariably appear in single basic colors with white markings limited to the face and legs. Browns, bays and blacks are most prevalent but there are some chestnuts, grays and roans. Most obvious, of course, is that by conformation, history and performance the Hackney is a highly refined and exclusive creature who is far more likely to interest the adult than the child.

The Shetland, Welsh, Connemara and Hackney are the most significant imports from the British Isles, but they are only a few of the pony breeds flourishing in that region. Still to be tapped by American horsemen are such strains as the Fell, the Highland, the New Forest, the Dale, not to mention the slightly more familiar Dartmoor and Exmoor types known for their iron constitution and, sometimes, a will to match. Another potential comer is the Icelandic pony. Descended from stock originally taken to Iceland by ninth century Norsemen, this generally tall, chestnut or reddish-colored strain is used in his homeland for the popular sport of trekking, or cross-country camping.

From the preceding it would seem that all the ponies in the United States are selective imports from afar. On the contrary, America does indeed possess wild native pony tribes of its own, but as we turn to consider these a curious fact will become apparent. Namely, while the United States has been in the forefront in developing such well-established breeds as the Morgan, the Saddle Horse, the Walker, the Quarter Horse—all of which have assumed a place of honor in the world's population of horses— it has tended to neglect its native pony stock altogether. Like ladies who look to Paris for trend-setting inspirations in dress, horsemen have eyed

The Hackney pony (below) is a miniature version of the Hackney horse (above). The Hackneys are the dandies of all the pony clans.

the foreign pony far more appreciatively than his own worthy and potentially valuable types. Hopefully, one day breeders will begin to turn their attentions in earnest to the development of domestic pony stock, and when this comes about they will be pleased to discover the good supply of raw material at hand.

A perfect example of overlooked potential is the Chincoteague pony whose home is the Assateague and Chincoteague Islands off the coast of Virginia. It is thought that these ponies are the descendants of Arab-blooded Spanish horses who escaped the wreckage of an ancient galleon and swam to safety on the islands. Made famous by Marguerite Henry's immortal children's story, *Misty of Chincoteague*, Chincoteagues still enjoy great publicity as a result of an annual Pony Penning Day ceremony in which the herds are rounded up and guided through the waters across the channel from Assateague to Chincoteague. An auction follows in which the foals are dispersed among the public.

Chincoteagues average about 12:2 to 13:2 hands and have all colors and combinations of spotting. The misfortune is that they mate freely, with better and poorer stock mixing at will. No organized effort has been made to improve the strain by establishment of an official register, stud book, and defined breed standards, so there is little uniform quality to the stock. They are considered crossbreds. There are, of course, individual Chincoteagues with handsome conformation, and their low, extended way of going makes these superior representatives ideal hunting ponies. But these well-endowed specimens are likely to have half brothers and sisters of a coarse and scruffy appearance. This is true of all feral ponies until some human controls are introduced to their breeding. It matters not a whit to the ponies, or to the buyer interested in a friendly, rugged pet, but a lack of breeding standards does take its toll in show competition where Chincoteagues do not cause as much of a stir as the imported strains which have prospered with just the slightest measure of human care.

Another domestic type that has been ignored is the Marsh Tacky—a wild race that roams the Carolinas and is reputed to be the untended offspring of stray Thoroughbred horse bands which wandered the territory after the Civil War. Tall, swift and still surprisingly refined after so many years of neglect, the Marsh Tacky is a superb hunter prospect. Yet he too, though a descendant of the mighty Thoroughbred, has not been made into a pure breed and is considered a crossbred. With no registry, no stud book, no organized program of improvement in effect, and none of the publicity that the Chincoteague has enjoyed, the Marsh Tacky is almost unknown outside his own part of the country.

Sea Island, Johns Island and doubtless other communities off the Atlantic coast also boast wild pony types whose possibilities have yet to be thoroughly explored and cultivated.

The feral strains should not feel singularly persecuted, because even the Kentucky Saddle Pony, an exact vest-pocket replica of the glorious full-

This Chincoteague pony could almost be a double for the immortal Misty.

grown Saddler, has also yet to be resolved into an official breed. Compact, rounded and shimmering, with arched neck and tail and bursting with all the exaggerated, electrifying action of his larger counterpart, the Saddle Pony is an ideal mount for the young saddle-seat equitation rider. Unlike the Chincoteague and Marsh Tacky, the Kentucky Saddle Pony did not arise in the wild and, in fact, is usually produced by crossing a pony mare or stallion with a full-sized Saddlebred horse. Until, through selective breeding, Saddle Ponies can be developed to reproduce faithfully among themselves and a stud book and registry can be established, they too will continue to fall into the crossbred category.

The solitary domestic American pony that exists as a specific pure breed, complete with official stud book, is the invention of one man—Mr. Leslie Boomhower of Mason City, Iowa. Known as the Pony of the Americas, this unique animal resulted entirely from an experiment that took place in 1956 in which Mr. Boomhower crossed a Shetland stallion with an Appaloosa mare. The outcome was so satisfactory that Mr. Boomhower resolved to produce his new creation in numbers and found a full-fledged breed.

The Shetland influence, of course, was responsible for the diminished size that created a pony—and no doubt added a measure of refinement and hardiness as well. But it was the Appaloosa infusion that introduced the exciting new aspect that was to become so appealing. Since the Appaloosa is a hereditary color breed, the mare transferred to her pony foal the eye-catching color pattern of her kind. Thus the Pony of the Americas is immediately recognized by the multitude of small, rounded, regularly-shaped spots that may spatter over his entire body or be confined to a blanket across the rump. Further traits peculiar to the strain are dark colorations, called "varnish" marks, which are about an inch in diameter and appear around the eyes, nose, mouth, jowls and under the tail. Sometimes the hooves are marked with a yellowish stripe. Measuring at maturity between 11:2 and 13 hands, the Pony of the Americas has become a great favorite in the West where he is regarded as the perfect cow pony for young, pint-sized ramrods.

In reviewing the entire subject of ponies, it is clear that there is one available for every taste, every use and every pocketbook. Price and pedigree make little difference in the love and pleasure that each of these types so willingly contributes, and for the horse lover who is still a bit hesitant about plunging in and buying a full-sized mount, the pony is an economical and instructive way to acquaint oneself with ownership. Once having overcome the initial nervousness that every new owner feels—no matter how few hands his purchase may measure—he will no longer hesitate to take his pick of the many magnificent breeds of horse which exist today for riders and horsemen of every interest.

Index

141